Canon EOS R100 User Guide

How To Master Your Camera Settings, Photo & Video Modes, and Autofocus with Step-by-Step Instructions for Beginners, Seniors & Creators

Randy Osborn

or website for the most current product specifications and instructions.

This guide is intended for educational and informational purposes only.

Table of Contents

Preface

Are you ready to finally take control of your Canon EOS R100 without feeling overwhelmed? Whether you're a complete beginner, a senior learning a new skill, or a content creator eager to master video, this all-in-one *Canon EOS R100 User Guide* is the ultimate step-by-step handbook you've been searching for.

Inside this *Canon R100 manual for beginners*, you'll find a clear, easy-to-understand approach to learning how to use Canon EOS R100 effectively—without the confusing jargon or information overload. This *Canon R100 camera book for seniors* and new users explains real-life camera settings and shooting recipes so you can capture beautiful images from day one.

From your first Canon R100 camera setup walkthrough to confidently navigating autofocus modes, ISO, shutter speed, and the exposure triangle, this guide covers it all. You'll learn exactly what each button, dial, and menu does with the help of an illustrated camera guide for new users, perfect for visual learners.

Whether you're into travel photography, family portraits, low-light photography, or creative shots, you'll uncover the best settings for Canon R100 beginners to make each photo count. We simplify Canon R100 settings explained—including Canon R100 settings for portraits, video resolution, face detection, frame rate, natural lighting, manual controls, lens basics, image stabilization, and more.

Want to create stunning video content? The *Canon EOS R100 autofocus and video guide* reveals how to shoot crisp, cinematic footage. Learn to shoot video with Canon R100 like a pro and use this *Canon R100 for YouTubers and vloggers* who want reliable quality. You'll even master audio input, lighting, and video stabilization in this easy Canon EOS camera tutorial.

We'll walk you through the *Canon Camera Connect app tutorial* and give you practical advice on photo transfer, backups, cloud sync, and mobile shooting. Whether you need a Canon camera connect app guide for fast sharing or simple setup, we've got you covered.

This isn't just another generic *Mirrorless Camera User Guide*. It's a Canon mirrorless camera for beginners companion filled with digital photography basics for beginners, photography tips and tricks, and step-by-step Camera guide strategies to unlock your camera's full potential.

You'll also get:

- A breakdown of RAW vs JPEG

- Best lenses and gear for Canon R100

- Smart file transfer and backup tips

- Easy photography tutorials for Canon EOS R100

- Real-world Canon R100 troubleshooting tips

- Fixes for blurry images, camera errors, and autofocus issues

- Canon R100 low light photography tricks

- How to avoid common beginner mistakes

- A full Canon mirrorless camera guide

Designed for those looking for an *easy Canon camera photography book* or the *best Canon R100 book for beginners*, this guide delivers. From vlogging with Canon cameras to shooting in golden hour, you'll gain confidence fast—without needing any editing software or prior photography experience.

Whether you're learning how to shoot with Canon R100 or just want a simple Canon camera setup step-by-step, this *Canon EOS R100 photography and video handbook* makes it painless. Packed with mirrorless camera photography tips, it's the definitive *Photography for Beginners Using Canon Cameras*—tailored to your lifestyle.

Introduction

In a world where cameras have grown increasingly complex—and even smartphones now boast more lenses than we can count—the Canon EOS R100 arrives like a breath of fresh air. It's not trying to be the most advanced mirrorless camera in the world. It doesn't come with a learning curve steep enough to make your head spin. Instead, Canon designed the R100 with one clear goal: to put professional-quality image-making within reach of everyday people.

This camera was built for the moments that matter—your child's first school play, the spontaneous road trip, the sunset you want to remember exactly as it felt. It's compact, lightweight, affordable, and powerful enough to shoot stunning images and crisp HD video. But here's the truth: even the most beginner-friendly camera can feel intimidating without the right guidance.

And that's where this book comes in.

Most user manuals are written by engineers, not photographers. They're filled with jargon, acronyms, and "tech-speak" that leave everyday users scratching their heads. You shouldn't need a PhD in digital imaging to take a decent photo of your daughter's graduation or your new puppy running through the yard.

This guide was written differently. It was created for real people who just want to pick up their camera and start capturing life—not decoding complicated menus or missing shots because of the wrong setting. Whether you're brand new to photography or stepping up from your smartphone, this book will help you master your Canon R100 with ease, confidence, and creativity.

Who This Book Is For

This book is for anyone who's ever said:

- "I just want to know which buttons to press."

- "Why are my photos always blurry?"

- "This camera has so many options—I don't know where to start."
- "I love photography, but I don't want to get overwhelmed by all the settings."

If that sounds like you, you're in the right place.

Whether you're a complete beginner, a returning hobbyist, a parent wanting better family pictures, a traveler documenting your adventures, or a YouTube creator looking for a compact camera with great video—the Canon R100 is a fantastic choice, and this guide was written with your exact needs in mind.

You don't need to know what ISO or metering means right now. You don't need to shoot in manual mode to get great results. What you need is a patient, clear, real-world walkthrough of your camera's most useful features—explained in plain English and tied to the kinds of photos and videos you actually want to take.

If you're looking for a book that empowers rather than overwhelms, you're holding it.

How to Use This Book (Quick Navigation for Real-Life Needs)

This guide is structured to help you get answers when you need them, not force you to read cover to cover like a textbook. While the chapters do build logically—starting with setup, then exploring shooting modes, focus, video, and troubleshooting—you're free to jump around based on what matters to you *today*.

Here's how to make the most of it:

- **Just got your camera out of the box?** Start with Chapter 1 for a smooth setup and to avoid common mistakes like improper lens mounting or SD card formatting errors.
- **Want to start shooting fast?** Flip to Chapter 3 to learn which shooting modes are best for portraits, pets, or travel.

- **Photos turning out blurry?** Head straight to Chapter 4 for focus tips and sharpness troubleshooting.

- **Ready to shoot video?** Chapter 7 breaks it down simply and shows you how to get the best results—even if you've never recorded a frame before.

- **Having tech problems?** Chapter 9 is your go-to resource for fixing common errors like battery drain, autofocus glitches, or camera freezing.

- **Looking to improve creatively?** Chapter 10 gives you everyday photography tips using the R100's strengths, even if you're not ready for full manual control yet.

Each chapter includes real-life examples, simplified settings recommendations, and visual explanations. There's no filler here— just real solutions to real questions. And in the back of the book, you'll find quick-reference tools like a camera setup cheat sheet, a menu map, and a glossary of terms you can actually understand.

Above all, this guide was written to give you something the Canon manual never could: confidence. Confidence to take your camera anywhere and trust that you know how to use it. Confidence to capture life as it unfolds—beautiful, unpredictable, and unrepeatable.

Let's get started.

Your camera is ready. And now, so are you.

Chapter 1

Unboxing and Setting Up the Canon EOS R100

Your camera journey begins here. Let's make sure your first steps are smooth, clear, and mistake-free.

What's in the Box (Explained in Plain English)

Let's start with the moment you lift the lid.

If you've just purchased your Canon EOS R100 and are unboxing it for the first time, you're probably staring at a neat arrangement of components, maybe a little excited… maybe a little intimidated. That's okay. Let's walk through it together.

Here's what should be inside your box:

- **Canon EOS R100 Camera Body** – This is the heart of your camera. It's what processes images, houses the sensor, and connects to your lens. It likely has a body cap on the front (a plastic disc covering the lens mount).

- **Canon RF-S 18–45mm Kit Lens** (if you bought the kit version) – This is a lightweight, general-purpose zoom lens. It's great for portraits, landscapes, and daily shooting.

- **LP-E17 Rechargeable Battery Pack** – The power source for your camera. Canon recommends only using their branded battery for safety and optimal performance.

- **Battery Charger LC-E17** – A wall plug-in charger. The battery slots in and clicks into place. No cords necessary— just plug the charger directly into a wall outlet.

- **Camera Strap** – It's not fancy, but it's important. This helps prevent the number one rookie mistake: dropping the camera while fumbling with buttons.

- **Printed Basic Manual or Quick Start Guide** – Usually a few pages, often in multiple languages. You can skip this in favor of this guide, which is far more user-friendly.

- **(Optional)** USB Cable or Lens Hood – Depending on your region or specific kit, you may also find a USB cable for data transfer and a lens hood (not always included).

Important: If anything is missing—especially the battery, charger, or lens—double-check your packaging material and reach out to your retailer immediately. Don't assume it's "hidden somewhere." Canon kits are usually tightly packed but thorough.

Battery Charging Do's and Don'ts

Before we even think about turning your camera on, let's talk about power.

DO charge your battery fully before first use.

Even if it shows some charge, a full charge ensures the battery is calibrated and ready for a long shoot.

To charge the battery:

1. Slide the battery into the charger until it clicks.

2. Plug the charger directly into a wall outlet.

3. The indicator light will be orange while charging and green when fully charged (or turn off, depending on the model).

DO: Always use Canon's original charger and battery.

DON'T: Leave the battery in a hot car or direct sunlight.

DON'T panic if it takes a while the first time.

It may take 2–3 hours to fully charge, depending on the remaining battery level.

DON'T use third-party batteries right away.

Generic batteries can save money but may trigger compatibility warnings or even damage your camera in the long run. If you choose to go third-party, do so only after you're fully familiar with your gear and know what brands are reputable.

Memory Card Must-Knows

Next up: memory. Your Canon EOS R100 doesn't have internal storage. You must insert a memory card to take or save photos.

Here's what you need:

- SD, SDHC, or SDXC memory card (UHS-I recommended) Look for Class 10 or higher. For video recording, especially at 1080p, speed matters.

Capacity Tip:

- 32GB is fine for beginners.
- 64GB–128GB gives you room to shoot more and worry less.

Installing the card:

1. Open the card/battery compartment (on the bottom of the camera).
2. Insert the card label-side facing the back of the camera.

3. Push gently until it clicks into place.

4. Close the door until it snaps shut.

DON'T force it. If it feels stuck, remove it and double-check the orientation.

ALWAYS format your new card inside the camera before your first use.

Formatting sets up the card correctly and clears any hidden data that might interfere.

To format:

- Menu > Wrench Tab (yellow) > Format Card

NEVER remove the card while the camera is writing or saving.

You could corrupt the card and lose your photos permanently.

Attaching the Kit Lens Properly (Solving

Common First-Time Mistakes)

Now, the part most beginners feel nervous about: putting the lens on.

Breathe. You've got this.

1. Remove the body cap from the camera (front) and the rear cap from the lens.
2. Line up the white square on the lens with the white square on the camera's lens mount.
3. Gently insert and rotate the lens clockwise until you hear a *click*.

DO NOT twist it backward or force it past the click.

Common Mistake: Some users forget to extend the 18–45mm lens before shooting.

Once attached, you'll need to twist the zoom ring to unlock and extend the lens. Until you do this, your screen will show a "Lens Retracted" warning.

Setting the Date/Time/Language

When you turn your camera on for the first time, you'll be prompted to set your language, time zone, and date/time.

It may seem minor, but don't skip it—your photo metadata (file info) and organizational tools rely on accurate timestamps.

1. Use the rear control dial or arrow buttons to set values.

2. Press SET to confirm.

3. Adjust for daylight savings time if needed.

TIP: If the camera keeps forgetting the date, your internal clock battery may be drained—this can happen if the camera sat in a warehouse for months. Recharging the main battery for a few hours often resolves it.

First-Time Power-On: What You'll See and What to Do

Okay, the lens is on. The battery is in. The card is inserted. It's go time.

Flip the ON/OFF switch to ON.

Here's what typically happens:

- The screen lights up.

- You may see a live view of what the camera is pointing at.

- If the lens is still retracted, you'll get a warning to extend it.

- If you're in Auto mode (green box on the dial), the camera will handle most settings for you.

From here, you're ready to:

- Take your first photo (half-press shutter to focus, full-press to shoot).

- Explore the Menu (tap the *Menu* button near the top-left).

- Review shots by pressing the Play button.

And just like that, you're ready to begin.

Solving the First-Time Frustrations (Real User Mistakes You'll Avoid Now)

- "My camera won't take photos!" → Extend the lens first.

- "Nothing saves to my card!" → Format the card in-camera.

- "Battery dies too fast!" → Charge fully before use. Don't leave Wi-Fi on when idle.

- "The screen is black!" → Lens cap still on? Or try Live View (press the DISP button).

- "Everything looks blurry!" → Chapter 4 has you covered—focus settings explained clearly.

What's in the Box

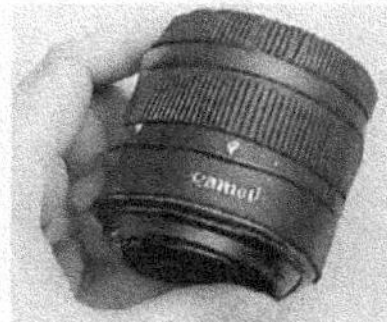

Charging the battery

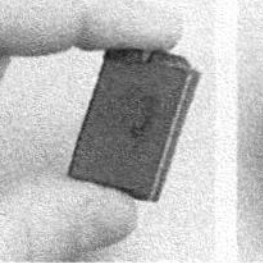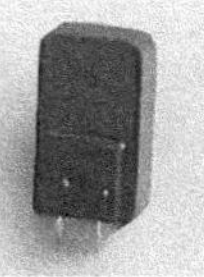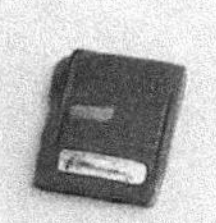

| Orange sure SD charging | Orargging Push gently. | Green iuṇtil it clicks. |

Insert your SD card

label side facing the LCD screen, Push gently until itck. Don't force it.

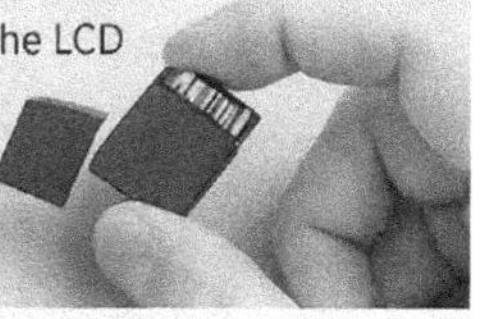

Mounting the Lens

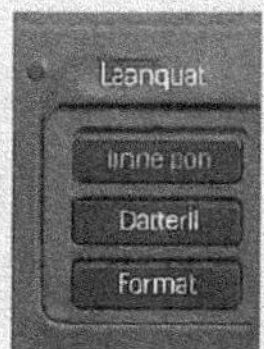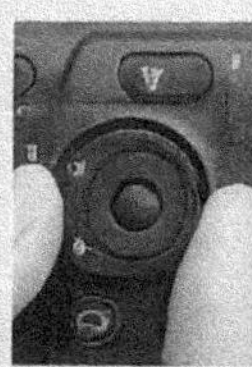

Align white jot on the lens with ◼ Ⅼoⴰ

Rotating Cl-lockwise until it clicks.

Extending the Lens

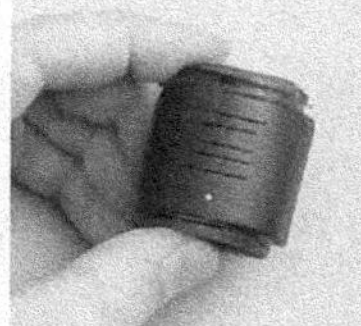

Check,, and act unḷḷ̇it oure fixé.

If the camera shows 'Lens retracted'.

Setting Date/Time/Language

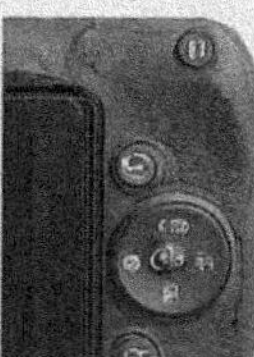

Language   Time zone   Date/time

If you see these messages, **don't panic.**
These are the must common beginner issues —
and all are easy fixes. You'll learn to read
your camera's cues quickly.

⚠ If you see messages, don't panic.

When powered on, you'll see what your lens sees.

If the lens is still retracted, extend it
before shooting. Use Auto mode to set
simply.

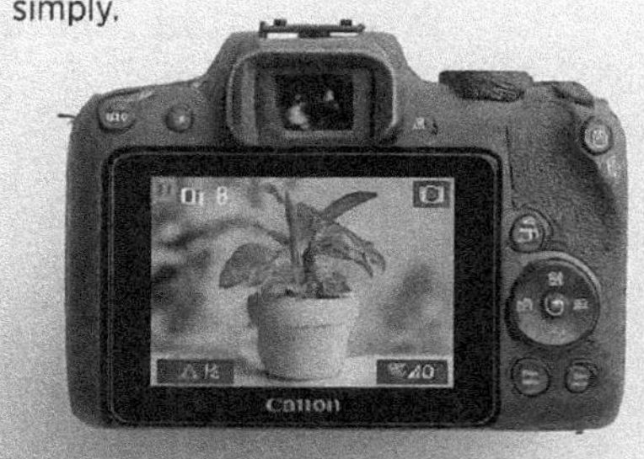

Chapter 2

Understanding the Buttons, Dials, and Menus

Learn your camera like it's a familiar tool—not a confusing machine.

Full Tour of the Body: Buttons, Ports, and What They Really Do

Let's be honest—if you've ever looked at the back of your Canon R100 and thought, *"I'm afraid to press anything,"* you're not alone.

The good news? This camera wasn't made to confuse you. You just need a simple orientation, like getting familiar with the dashboard of a car. Once you know where things are—and what *not* to worry about—you'll feel a whole lot more in control.

Let's walk through the Canon R100 body together, one side at a time.

Top of the Camera – Where Shooting Begins

- **Power Switch (ON/OFF):** Located around the shutter button. Flip it right to turn the camera on, left to turn it off. Simple.

- **Shutter Button:** Press halfway to focus, all the way down to take a photo. You'll use this more than anything else.

- **Mode Dial (Big Rotating Wheel):** This selects your shooting mode (Auto, Manual, Video, etc.). More on this in Chapter 3.

- **Main Dial (Near the Shutter Button):** This little wheel changes settings depending on the mode you're in—like aperture or shutter speed.

Pro Tip: When in doubt, leave the mode dial on the green "A+" (Auto) icon—your camera will do the thinking for you.

Back of the Camera – Your Control Center

- **LCD Screen:** Your digital window. Shows your settings, previews shots, and displays menus.

- **Menu Button (Top-Left):** Opens the full settings menu.

- **Info Button (Next to Menu):** Cycles through what information is shown on-screen.

- **D-Pad (Four Arrows with SET in the Center):** Navigates menus and moves your focus point.

- **Playback Button (▶):** Lets you review your photos and videos.

- **Trash/Delete Button (🗑):** Deletes selected files (only after confirmation).

- **DISP Button:** Toggles different viewing options while shooting.

- **AF (Auto Focus) Button:** Quick access to autofocus modes.

Don't worry about pressing the wrong thing. You can't break the camera with a button press. Anything you change can be reset.

Left Side of the Camera – Your Connection Hub

- **Microphone Jack:** Plug in an external mic for better audio when shooting video.

- **HDMI Port:** Output to a monitor or TV.

- **USB Port:** Use it to transfer files or connect to a computer.

These ports are tucked under a rubber flap. Be gentle when opening it—don't yank.

Bottom of the Camera – The Powerhouse

- **Battery Compartment:** This is also where the SD card goes. Slide to open. The battery only fits one way—don't force it.

If you plan to shoot for long sessions, invest in a spare battery. It's one of the best accessories you can buy.

Menu Navigation 101: How to Actually Find

What You Need

The Canon R100 menu system is like a well-organized filing cabinet—but only if you know where to look. Let's break it down.

When you press the Menu button, you'll see tabs across the top. Each tab contains a few pages of related settings.

Here's what they mean:

Shooting Tab (Red Camera Icon)

Everything related to how the camera captures images:

- Image quality (RAW, JPEG)

- Drive mode (single shot, burst)

- Self-timer

- White balance

- Metering mode

Use this tab when you're adjusting how your photo is taken.

Movie Tab (Red Camera with Video Icon)

This only appears in movie mode. Controls:

- Video quality (Full HD, 4K)

- Frame rate

- Microphone levels

Use when filming video.

Setup Tab (Yellow Wrench Icon)

General system settings:

- Date/time

- File numbering

- Format card

- LCD brightness

- Auto power off

This is where you go to "fix stuff" or do general housekeeping.

Custom Functions (Orange)

Advanced tweaks for autofocus, button behavior, etc.

If this feels confusing, skip it for now. Not necessary for everyday shooting.

My Menu (Green Star Tab)

This one's a game-changer—more on that below.

Menu Navigation Tips:

- Use the left/right arrows to move between tabs.

- Use the up/down arrows to scroll within each tab.

- Press SET to open or confirm an option.

- Press MENU again to exit.

The "My Menu" Tab – Your Secret Shortcut

Now, here's a feature most beginners don't use—but absolutely should.

The My Menu tab (green star icon) is your custom dashboard. It lets you *bookmark* your most-used settings, so you don't have to hunt through the full menu every time.

Here's how to set it up:

1. Go to the My Menu tab (far right).

2. Select "Add My Menu Tab"

3. Choose "Register to My Menu"

4. Add items like:

    o   Format card

    o   Image quality

    o   White balance

    o   Wi-Fi connection

    o   Auto power-off

Now, when you press Menu, you can jump straight to the things *you actually use*—saving time and frustration.

Think of My Menu like a favorite playlist. Put your most-used settings there and skip the digging.

Customizing Controls for Simpler Use

One of the best things about the Canon R100 is that it grows with you.

As you get more comfortable, you'll want to make the camera feel more like an extension of *you*. And that's where custom controls come in.

Here's how to start:

1. Reassigning the Main Dial

Want to change which setting the dial controls in manual mode? You can.

- Menu > Custom Functions > Operation/Others > Dial Function

2. Customizing the Set Button

You can make the SET button quickly access ISO, white balance, or other favorites.

- Menu > Custom Functions > Customize Buttons

▢ 3. Simplify Your Display

Too much info on the screen? Change the display style.

- Menu > Shooting Tab > Screen Info Settings

These aren't mandatory—but they can make your experience more fluid as your skills grow.

Recap: Problems Solved in This Chapter

- **"What do all these buttons do?"** → You now know each button and its purpose, in plain English.
- **"Menus are overwhelming!"** → You've got a simple map to navigate them like a pro.

- **"Where are the settings I use most?"** → They live in your *My Menu* tab now.

- **"How do I make the camera easier to use?"** → You've started customizing controls to match your style.

You don't need to memorize everything in one sitting. This chapter is here for reference any time your hands feel unsure. Like any tool, the more you use it, the more natural it becomes.

In the next chapter, we'll break down shooting modes—and finally answer that common question:

"What's the difference between Auto, Manual, and everything in between?"

Let's take the mystery out of the mode dial.

UNDERSTANDING THE BUTTONS, DIALS, AND MENUS

FULL TOUR OF THE CAMERA BODY

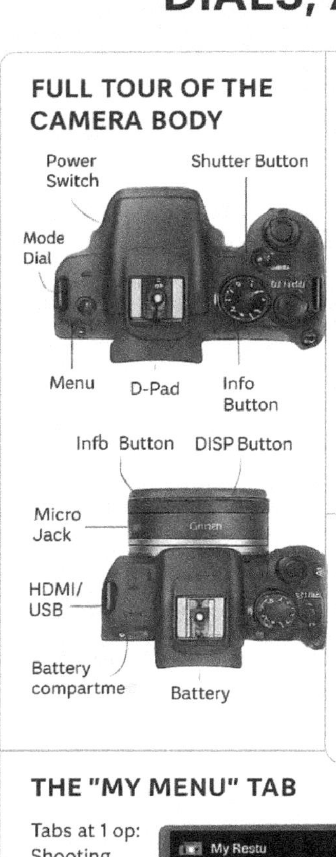

MENU NAVIGATION 101

Tab at to 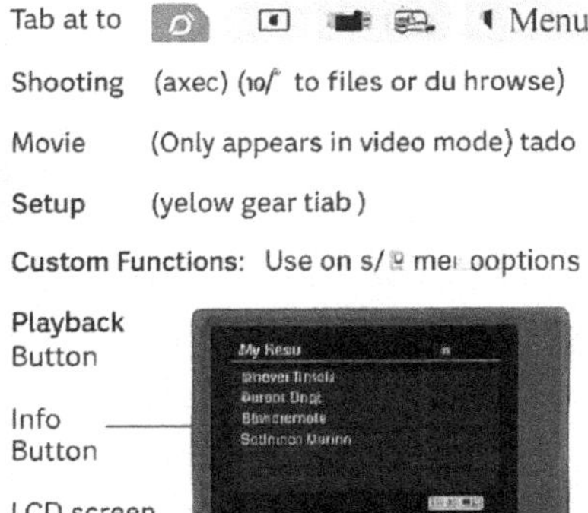 Menu

Shooting (axec) (\o/ to files or du hrowse)

Movie (Only appears in video mode) tado

Setup (yelow gear tiab)

Custom Functions: Use on s/ mei ooptions

Playback Button

Info Button

LCD screen

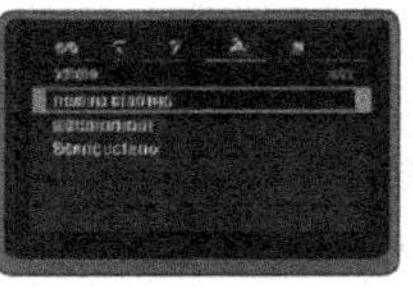

THE "MY MENU" TAB

Organize your green menu soptions -- in the green tab.

Use these tab to forqucky ascet ISO. focus, or others.

THE "MY MENU" TAB

Tabs at 1 op: Shooting mode

Manual time (est.)

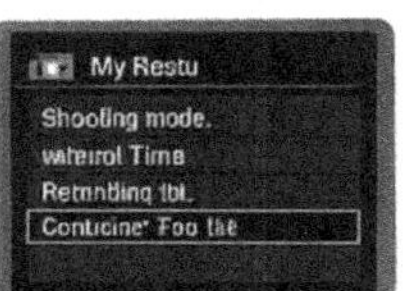

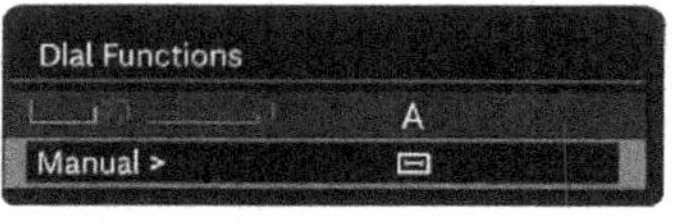

Assaign your Get button

CUSTOMIZIG CONTROLS

Reassign one with Main °

Assign SET to quickly ac- case ISO, focus or other

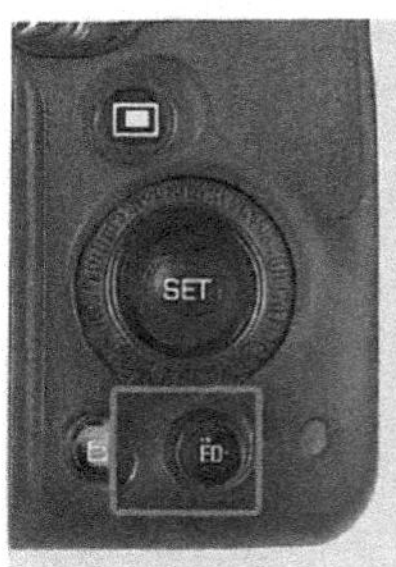

Chapter 3

Mastering Shooting Modes Made Simple

Your camera has more to offer than Auto. Let's unlock it—at your pace.

If you've been living in "Auto mode," there's nothing wrong with that.

Scene Intelligent Auto (that green box on your Canon R100's mode dial) is like cruise control. It handles the gears for you, makes sure you don't stall, and generally keeps things safe and easy.

But sooner or later, you'll take a photo where Auto just doesn't get it right—maybe your subject's face is blown out by the sun, or the background is sharp while your child's face is fuzzy. That's the moment every photographer realizes: *I need to understand how my camera thinks.*

Good news: you don't have to learn everything at once. In this chapter, we're going to break down each shooting mode—clearly, visually, and without jargon—and show you when it's actually worth making the switch.

Scene Intelligent Auto vs. Creative Assist

Let's start with the two beginner-friendly modes you've probably seen already: Scene Intelligent Auto and Creative Assist.

Scene Intelligent Auto (A+ mode)

- Marked by a green "A+" icon on your mode dial.
- The camera does *everything*—exposure, focus, white balance, and even chooses a "scene type" (portrait, landscape, etc.) based on what it sees.

When to use it:

- You're in a rush or unsure what you're shooting.

- Lighting is unpredictable.

- You're just starting out and want decent photos without adjusting settings.

Limitations:

- No creative control.

- Can misread scenes (e.g., backlit subjects often come out dark).

- You can't adjust how blurry the background looks.

Creative Assist Mode

Think of this as training wheels for manual photography.

- Available via touchscreen when in Auto or Scene modes.

- Instead of using camera terms like "aperture" or "exposure compensation," it lets you adjust your image using friendly sliders:

  o Brightness

- o Background blur

- o Color tone

- o Vividness

When to use it:

- You want to experiment with your photo's look but still want the camera to do most of the technical work.

This is the perfect "next step" after Auto.

Program (P), Aperture Priority (Av), Shutter Priority (Tv), Manual (M) Modes Explained

These four modes are where your creative journey really begins. Let's decode them with real-life examples so you'll know exactly *when* to use which.

Program Mode (P) – *"Almost Auto, but Smarter"*

- The camera chooses aperture and shutter speed for you, but *you* can still change ISO, white balance, picture style, and exposure compensation.

- Ideal for casual shooting when you want some say in the final look.

Example use: Shooting indoors with mixed lighting, and you want to warm up the colors or brighten the image a bit.

Aperture Priority (Av) – *"Control the Blur"*

- You choose the aperture (f-number), and the camera adjusts the shutter speed automatically.

- A lower f-number = more background blur (great for portraits).

- A higher f-number = more in focus (great for landscapes).

When to use it:

- Portraits with creamy background (f/4 or lower)

- Travel photos where you want both the subject and background in focus (f/8–f/11)

- Food and product shots

This is the most popular mode among photographers—easy and powerful.

Shutter Priority (Tv) – *"Freeze or Blur the Motion"*

- You choose the shutter speed, and the camera adjusts the aperture.

- Use a fast shutter speed to freeze motion (1/500s or faster).

- Use a slow shutter speed to create blur (1/30s or slower).

When to use it:

- Pets or kids running (use 1/1000s or faster)

- Waterfalls, light trails, or motion blur (try 1/15s or slower with a tripod)

- Indoor sports or action scenes

Manual Mode (M) – *"You're in Charge"*

- You set everything: shutter speed, aperture, ISO.

- Best when lighting is tricky or consistent—like studio work or night photography.

When to use it:

- Shooting fireworks, stars, or long exposures

- You want full creative control

- You're using flash or studio lighting setups

Don't be afraid of Manual Mode. Start using it once you understand how shutter, aperture, and ISO work together (we'll cover that triangle in Chapter 5).

When and Why to Switch Modes

Now that you understand what each mode does, here's a simple rule:

Switch modes when your photos don't match your intention.

If you:

- Want a blurry background but Auto keeps everything sharp → Switch to Av mode

- Keep getting blurry action shots of your dog → Try Tv mode with a fast shutter speed

- Need consistent brightness in tricky lighting → Use M mode

- Are happy with the results and just want to practice → Stick with P or Creative Assist

Think of each mode as a tool—not a test. There's no "right" or "wrong" mode. Just the one that matches the moment.

Best Starter Mode for Each Scenario

Here's your quick-start cheat sheet—because knowing *when* to use a mode is half the battle.

Portraits

Use: Av Mode, f/2.8 to f/4

Why: You get beautiful blur behind your subject and soft focus on the face.

Travel or Landscape

Use: Av Mode, f/8 to f/11

Why: Keeps the whole scene sharp, from foreground to background.

Pets & Action

Use: Tv Mode, 1/1000s or faster

Why: Freezes motion so you don't get blur from movement.

Food or Product Shots

Use: Av Mode, f/2.8 for dramatic depth

Why: Makes the food or object pop against a soft background.

Video

Use: Movie Mode (Manual or Auto)

Tips:

- Set shutter speed to 1/50 for a natural look

- Use Servo AF for smooth focus tracking

- Keep ISO low to reduce grain

Final Word: Don't Let the Dial Intimidate You

Every pro photographer started where you are—looking at the mode dial and wondering what would happen if they turned it out of Auto. They didn't get better because they memorized manuals. They got better because they practiced with purpose.

So try this:

- Spend one afternoon shooting only in Av mode.

- Take portraits of your family or flowers.

- Then try the same shots in Auto.

- Compare. Learn. Adjust.

It's not about perfection—it's about exploration. The Canon R100 is your creative partner, not your critic.

Mastering Shooting Modes Made Simple

Scene Intelligent Auto

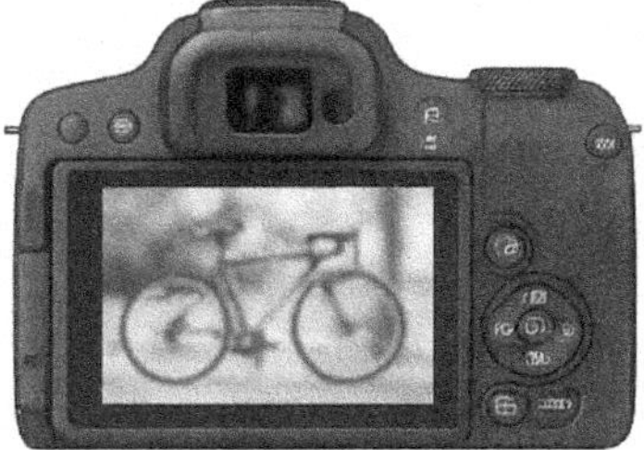

Camera fully automatic

Creative Assist

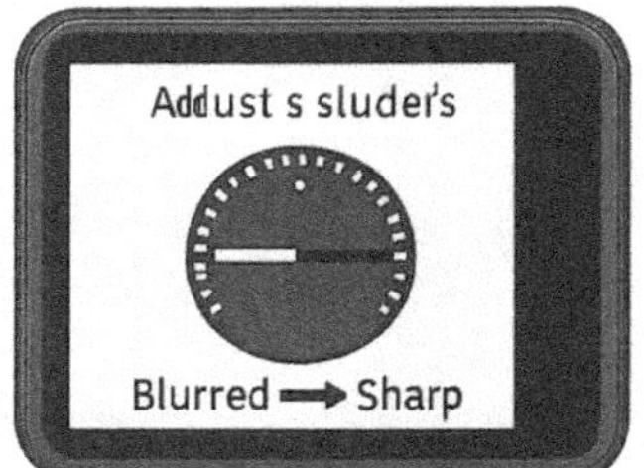

Adjust on sliders

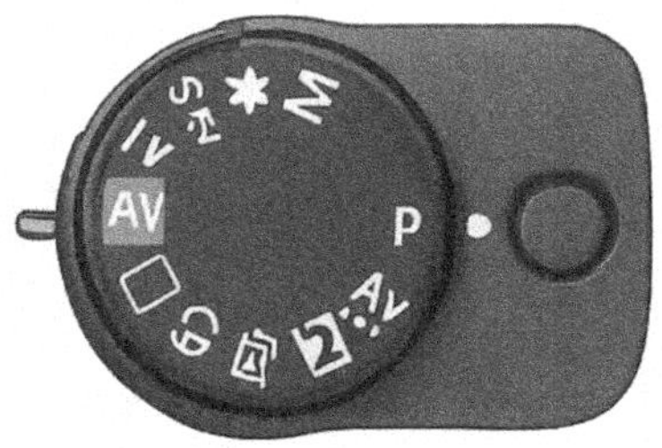

Program (P) Camera the exposure, you can adjust some settings

Av Aperture Priority (Av)
You control the f-stop, camera sets the **shutter** speed

P Program
Camera sets the exposure. you can adjust some settings

Tv Shutter Priority (Tv)
You control the shutter speed camera sets the aperture

Best Starter Mode for Each Scenario

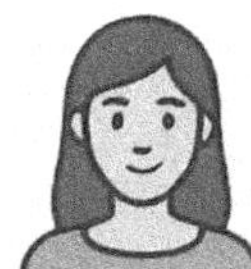

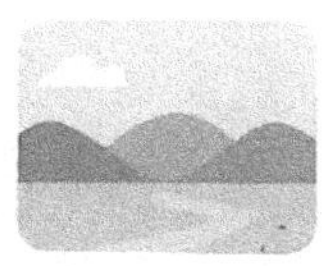

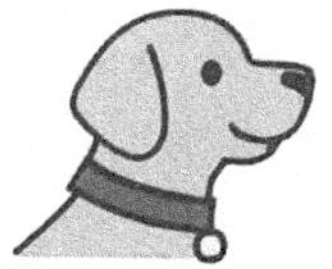

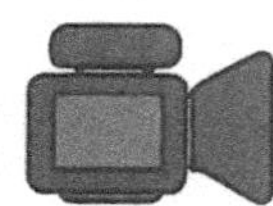

Portraunt
Av Mode
f/2.8 to f4

Travel or lands-
Av Mode
f/8 to f11

Pets & action
Tv Mode
1/1000s or faster

Video
Movie Mode
Use Servo AF

Chapter 4

Focus, Sharpness & Blurry Photo Fixes

Let's make every photo come out just as clear as the moment it captures.

You press the shutter. The moment feels perfect. But when you review the shot, something's wrong.

Your subject is blurry. The background's sharp. Or worse—*everything* looks a little off. It's frustrating, isn't it?

You may start wondering if it's the lens, the camera, or you. But here's the good news: it's probably just your focus settings, and once you understand how they work, you'll never have to guess again.

The Canon EOS R100 has a solid autofocus system, but like any smart tool, it needs to be told what you want. This chapter will teach you how to communicate with your camera clearly, so it knows exactly what to focus on—and when.

Understanding Autofocus: One-Shot, Servo, Manual

There are three main focus modes on your Canon R100, and they each have a specific job.

Let's break them down with real-world examples.

One-Shot AF

Think: *Still subjects*—like a posed portrait, a landscape, or a product on a table.

- Press the shutter halfway, and the camera locks focus on your subject.
- Once it's locked, it won't adjust if the subject moves.
- Best when your subject—and you—are standing still.

Use for:

Portraits, still life, food photography, street shots when your subject is stationary.

Servo AF (Continuous)

Think: *Moving subjects*—like your child running, a dog chasing a ball, or someone walking toward you.

- The camera continues tracking your subject *while* you hold the shutter halfway down.
- It adjusts focus as the subject moves.

Use for:

Action shots, kids and pets, sports, candid walking portraits.

Manual Focus

Think: *You want full control* or the camera can't lock focus properly.

- You switch the lens or camera to MF (Manual Focus), then twist the focus ring yourself.

- Often used for macro, low-light, or artistic control.

Use for:

Macro photography, low-light static scenes, or when autofocus struggles (e.g., through glass or in very dark rooms).

How to switch focus mode:

Go to Menu > Shooting Tab > AF Operation, or press the **AF** button on the back for quick access.

Solving "Why is My Photo Blurry?" Step-by-Step

Let's fix the single most common complaint with beginner photos: blurriness.

Here's your step-by-step troubleshooting guide:

1. Is the camera shaking?

Hold your camera steady. Shaky hands at slower shutter speeds = blurry results.

🔧 Fix:

- Use a shutter speed of at least 1/60s for still subjects.
- For action, go faster: 1/500s or more.

2. Is your subject moving?

If you're using One-Shot AF, it locks focus—but won't track movement. So if your subject moves after focus, they'll be out of focus.

🔧 Fix:

- Switch to Servo AF for moving subjects.

3. Is autofocus choosing the wrong part of the scene?

Cameras don't read minds. If you're in Auto AF, the R100 might lock onto the *background* instead of your subject.

🔧 **Fix:**

- Use Face + Eye Tracking or tap the subject on the LCD (in Live View).
- Switch to Spot AF or Zone AF and move the focus point manually.

4. Are you too close to your subject?

Lenses have a minimum focusing distance. Get too close and it won't focus at all.

🔧 **Fix:**

- Back up a bit.
- For close-ups, try a macro lens or crop in later.

5. Is your aperture too wide (too low)?

Wide apertures (like f/1.8 or f/2.8) have a *very shallow* depth of field. Only a small slice of your subject will be in focus.

🛠 **Fix:**

- Try f/4 or f/5.6 for more focus depth.

- Focus carefully on the **eye** if shooting portraits.

Face Detection and Eye Tracking Tips

Your Canon R100 comes with Face + Eye Detection AF, which is a gift for beginners—if you enable it.

Here's how it works:

- The camera automatically finds human faces in the frame.

- It prioritizes the eye closest to the lens for sharpest focus.

- It even tracks as the person moves.

To enable it:

Go to Menu > AF Tab > Subject to Detect > People

Then AF Method > Face + Tracking

Tips for Better Results:

- Use Servo AF with Face Tracking for kids and pets on the move.

- In bright light, make sure your subject's face isn't in shadow—Face Detection works best with clear facial features.

- If the camera can't find the eye, it will default to face or body.

Great for: Portraits, street photography, events, or vlogging.

Manual Focus Help for Beginners

Manual focus can feel intimidating at first—but sometimes, it's the only way to get the shot.

Let's say you're photographing:

- A product through a shop window

- A flower in dim light

- Something very small or detailed

Autofocus might "hunt" back and forth and never lock in. That's when Manual Focus (MF) shines.

How to Use Manual Focus:

1. Switch your lens to MF (there may be a tiny switch on the lens itself).

2. Look through the viewfinder or LCD.

3. Turn the focus ring until your subject looks sharp.

Tip:

Enable MF Peaking (if supported) in your Canon menu. It highlights the areas in focus with a colored outline—very helpful for beginners.

AF Settings for Moving Subjects

Trying to photograph a toddler on the move or a pet chasing a ball?

You'll need your camera's autofocus to think fast.

Here's how to set it up:

Best R100 AF Settings for Action:

1. **AF Operation:** Servo AF

   o   Keeps adjusting focus while subject moves.

2. **AF Method: Face + Tracking** or Zone AF

   o   Face tracking for people

   o   Zone AF for fast, random movement (pets, sports)

3. **Drive Mode: High-Speed Continuous**

   o   Press and hold shutter for a burst of images—better chance one is perfectly in focus.

4. **Shutter Speed:**

   o   Use 1/1000s or faster for running subjects.

5. **Lens Tip:**

    o Turn off image stabilization (IS) only if using a tripod. Otherwise, leave it ON for handheld shots.

Bonus: Use Back-Button Focus (assign AF to a separate button) if you want even better control while tracking subjects. More on that in the customization chapter.

Final Word: Your Focus Is Now Clear

Focus isn't just technical—it's emotional.

When you nail it, the image connects. The child's eye is sharp. The dog's leap is frozen mid-air. The memory *feels* alive.

And now, you know how to make that happen.

Here's a final reminder:

- For still scenes → One-Shot AF
- For motion → Servo AF

- For faces → Face + Eye Tracking

- For tough situations → Manual Focus

- And when in doubt → Tap the screen to focus where *you* want

FUCUSSTANDING AUTOFOCUS: ONE-SHOT, SERVO, MANUAL

SOLVING 'WHY IS MY PHOTO BLURRY?' STEP-STP

1. One-Shot AF
Locks focus on still subjects (e.g. porfraits)

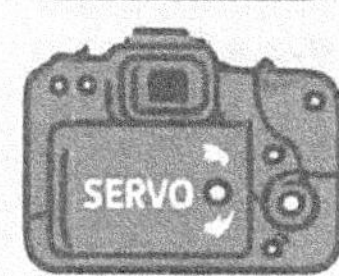

2. Servo AF
(AI Servo)
Tracks moving subjects

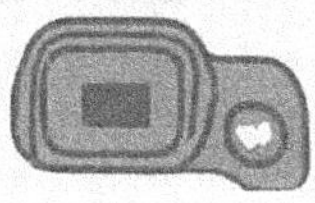

3. Manual Focus
Confirm focus point on subject

SOLVING 'WHY IS MY PHOTO BLURRY?'
STEP-BY-STEP

1. Is f camera shaking?
Use a faster **speed**
(e.g. 1/500 sec)

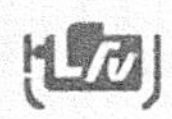
Servo

2. Is f subject moving?
Use Servo AF

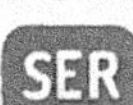

3. Is focus on a errors?
Confirm focus point

4. Is aperture 'x' too low (f/1.8)
Use a higher f-stop (f.4 or f5.6

AF SETTINGS FOR MOVING SUBJECTS

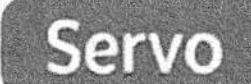  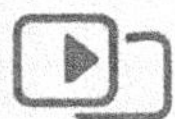

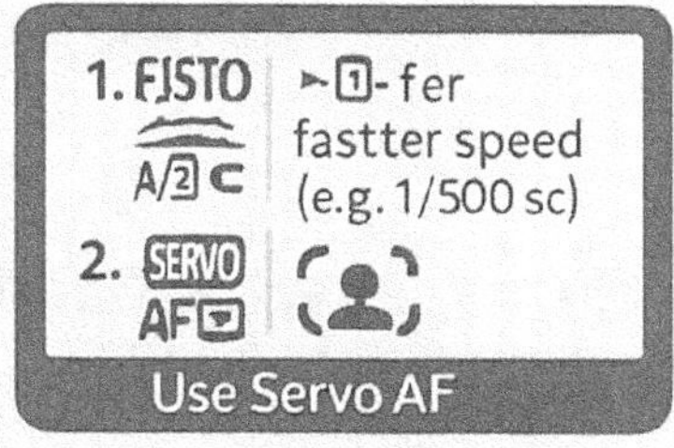

Fix at corect/confiirim

4. Is focus too low (f/1.8)
Use higher f-stop (f.4

FACE DETECTION AND EYE TRACKING TIPS

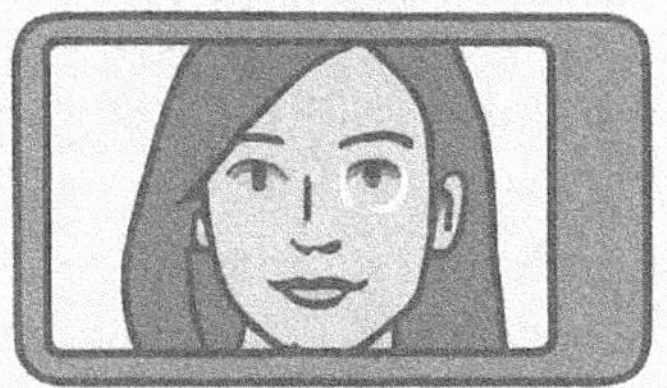

Enable face & eve detection in the AF menu

MANUAL FOCUS HELP FOR BEGINNERS

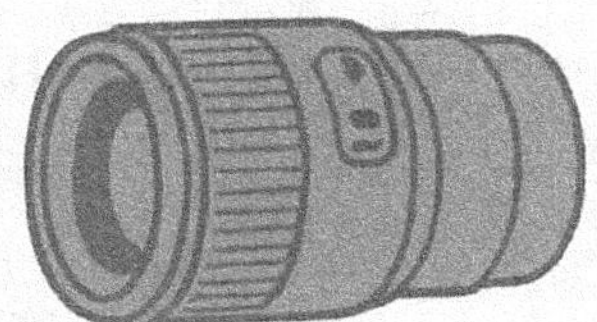

Use the focus ring on the lens

Chapter 5

Exposure Made Easy

ISO, Aperture & Shutter Speed—Demystified for Real-World Photography

Let's begin with this truth: great photos aren't about fancy gear. They're about understanding *light*.

Whether you're photographing your child blowing out birthday candles, or capturing golden sunlight falling through trees at sunset, what your camera is really doing is collecting light—and *how* it collects light is what we call exposure.

What Exposure Means (with Real-Life Analogies)

Exposure simply refers to how bright or dark your photo turns out.

But let's take it out of the technical box for a second. Imagine you're filling a glass of water. If you:

- **Pour too little** → the glass is underfilled (underexposed = too dark)

- **Pour too much** → the glass overflows (overexposed = too bright)

- **Get it just right** → perfect exposure

Now imagine that the water pressure, size of the faucet, and how long you let it run *all affect how much water goes in the glass*. That's exactly how ISO, aperture, and shutter speed work.

They're the three tools that control how much light hits your camera sensor:

- Aperture = Faucet opening (How wide the lens opens)

- Shutter Speed = How long it stays open

- ISO = The sensitivity of your sensor (how "thirsty" your sensor is)

Together, they form the Exposure Triangle. Let's unpack each one clearly and practically—so you know how to use them *without guessing.*

How to Stop Overexposure in Bright Light

This is one of the most common issues beginners run into. You go outside, take a photo on a sunny day, and boom—your subject is totally washed out. The sky is a blown-out white mess, and everyone's faces are pale and detail-less.

What to do:

1. **Lower your ISO**

   o   ISO 100 is ideal for bright conditions.

   o   The lower the ISO, the less sensitive the camera is to light.

2. **Increase your shutter speed**

   o   Try 1/1000s or faster in full daylight.

- o A fast shutter speed lets in less light, helping prevent overexposure.

3. **Narrow your aperture (higher f-number)**

   - o f/8 to f/11 helps control excess light.

4. **Use Exposure Compensation (+/- button)**

   - o In Auto or Semi-Auto modes, press the "+/-" button and dial left to darken the photo slightly.

Real-Life Fix: Shooting at the beach or in snow? Use ISO 100, shutter speed 1/2000s, and f/11. Also, consider turning on "Highlight Alert" in your Canon R100 so the camera warns you when parts of your photo are too bright.

Low-Light Shooting Without a Tripod

Let's flip the situation.

You're indoors at night, or outside trying to capture a cozy street scene. You take a shot, and it turns out *blurry* or *grainy* or both.

What happened?

Your camera needs *more light*, but it can't hold still long enough—
or it's compensating in the wrong way.

What to do:

1. **Raise your ISO**

    o   ISO 800 to 3200 is often necessary indoors.

    o   Be cautious: higher ISO can introduce grain (called
    "noise").

2. **Widen your aperture (lower f-number)**

    o   f/2.8 lets in much more light than f/8.

    o   This gives you better low-light performance and
    shallower depth of field.

3. **Use a slower shutter speed—but not too slow**

    o   1/60s is about the slowest handheld speed for sharp
    photos.

    o   If your subject is still, try 1/30s—but hold very
    steady.

Real-Life Fix: Shooting candlelit dinners or night portraits? Try ISO 1600, f/2.8, and 1/60s. Brace your elbows, lean on a chair, or use a wall to stay steady.

When to Adjust ISO vs. Shutter Speed

Now you might be wondering: *Which setting do I change first?*

Here's a practical cheat sheet based on what kind of issue you're solving:

If your photo is too dark:

- Increase ISO (up to 1600 or 3200 if needed)
- Or slow down your shutter speed (but don't go below 1/60s if handheld)

If your photo is too bright:

- Lower ISO to 100
- Increase shutter speed (1/500s or faster)

- Or use a narrower aperture (f/8–f/11)

If your subject is moving and blurry:

- Raise shutter speed (try 1/1000s or higher)

- Then raise ISO if photo becomes too dark

If your subject is still but photo is grainy:

- Lower ISO (to reduce grain)

- Widen your aperture (f/2.8 or f/4)

- Use a tripod if you need a slower shutter speed

Tip: Your Canon R100 has a feature called "Auto ISO." In most modes, this lets the camera adjust ISO while you focus on aperture or shutter. It's a great helper while learning.

Simple Guide to the Exposure Triangle with

R100 Defaults

Here's a snapshot of how the three exposure elements work together—and what default ranges work well on the Canon EOS R100.

Aperture (f-stop)

- Controls: How much light enters through the lens

- Also affects: Depth of field (how much of the image is in focus)

- Use:

    - f/2.8–f/4 for portraits (blurry background)

    - f/8–f/11 for landscapes (sharp all over)

Shutter Speed

- Controls: How long the shutter stays open

- Also affects: Motion blur or sharpness

- Use:

- o   1/1000s for action

- o   1/60s for handheld shots

- o   Slower only with tripod

ISO

- Controls: How sensitive your sensor is to light

- Also affects: Noise level (grain)

- Use:

  - o   ISO 100 for sunny days

  - o   ISO 800–1600 indoors

  - o   ISO 3200+ only if needed (with some grain)

Canon R100 Defaults to Remember:

- Auto ISO range: 100–6400

- Lowest native ISO: 100

- Max shutter speed: 1/4000s

- Lowest aperture depends on lens (e.g., f/4.5 on the kit lens)

Final Thoughts: Learning to See Light

Exposure isn't just a technical setting—it's how you tell stories with light.

Once you understand how ISO, aperture, and shutter speed work together, you can *shape* your photo instead of just reacting to it. You'll be able to:

- Choose what's sharp or soft

- Decide what motion to freeze or blur

- Brighten or darken scenes intentionally

Start small. Practice with one setting at a time. Shoot the same scene at three different ISOs. Try different f-stops in the same light. Look at what changes. Then do it again tomorrow.

And remember: you're not just learning settings. You're learning *vision*.

Exposure controls how bright or dark a photo is

Underexposed
too dark

Overexposed
too bright

Exposure Triangle

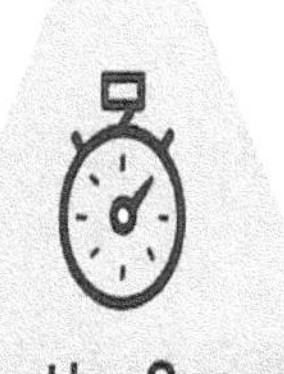

Shutter Speed
Controls how long
ligt hits sensor

How to stop overexposure in bright light

1. Lower (50 (eg., 100)
2. Make shutter speed faster
3. Make aperture narrower (higher f-stop)

Use exposure compensation

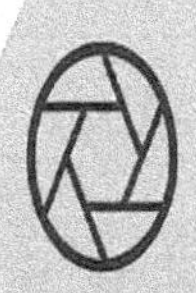

Sets sensitivity
to light

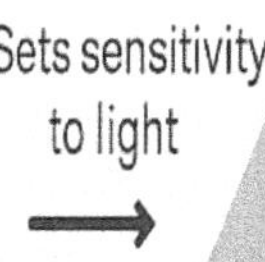

Aperture
(f-stop)
Controls amount of light

ISO
Sets sensitivity to light

Appuer oxpaned

- Use f/2.8 – f/ 4 for portraits (blurry background)
- Use f/8 – f/11 for landscapes
  [sh erty aff ruued]

Low-light shooting without a tripod

- Raise ISO
- Use a wide aperture (low f-stop)

Chapter 6

Picture Styles, White Balance & Creative Looks

Color is emotion. This chapter shows you how to make your photos feel alive—right out of the camera.

Have you ever looked at a photo you just took and thought, *"Why doesn't this look like what I saw with my eyes?"* Maybe the sky came out too blue. Skin tones looked strange. Or the whole image felt…flat.

It's not your fault. Cameras don't see like we do. But the Canon EOS R100 gives you powerful tools to help your camera interpret the world the way *you* experience it.

In this chapter, you'll learn how to shape the visual personality of your photos using Picture Styles, tweak colors with White Balance, and even apply creative effects—all without touching editing software.

This is where technical settings start to feel like artistic choices. Let's make your images match your memories.

Choosing the Best Picture Style (Standard, Portrait, Landscape, etc.)

The Canon R100 comes with a built-in palette of **Picture Styles**— think of them like different film types from the old days. Each style adjusts your photo's color tone, contrast, sharpness, and saturation.

And the best part? You can apply them before you take the shot. That means less time editing later.

Here are the main ones you'll use:

Standard (Default)

- Balanced for most situations

- Good for general shooting

- Slight contrast and sharpening

  Use for: Everyday snapshots, travel, family

Portrait

- Softer skin tones, less contrast

- Flatter shadows, gentle highlights

  Use for: Close-ups of people, headshots, kids

Landscape

- Punchier blues and greens

- Boosted contrast and saturation

  Use for: Nature scenes, architecture, outdoor vistas

Neutral

- Very little processing

- Flat and soft, great for editing later

  Use for: When you plan to edit your photos manually

Faithful

- Reproduces colors exactly as they appear under daylight

- Slightly warmer than Neutral

  Use for: Product photography or accurate color work

Monochrome

- Black-and-white with optional filters (red, yellow, green)

  Use for: Timeless, emotional portraits or dramatic lighting

To change Picture Style:

Menu > Shooting Tab > Picture Style

(or tap the Q/Quick menu on the back LCD)

Customizing Styles for Your Taste

Each Picture Style comes with adjustable settings:

- Sharpness

- Contrast

- Saturation

- Color tone

This means you can fine-tune any style to suit your eye. For instance:

- Want punchier portraits? Add +1 sharpness, +1 contrast

- Want softer, pastel-like images? Drop contrast and saturation slightly

- Want film-like colors? Use Neutral with slightly lowered sharpness and saturation

Tip: You can save your favorite custom setup under a User Defined Picture Style.

This lets you create your own look—so every photo you shoot has *your* fingerprint on it.

Fixing Weird Colors with White Balance

Let's talk about the silent photo killer: weird color casts.

Sometimes your camera's "Auto White Balance" (AWB) guesses wrong. Maybe a photo looks too orange indoors or too blue in the shade. That's because white balance tells your camera what *color* light you're shooting in—and if it's off, everything looks unnatural.

Common White Balance Settings:

- **Auto WB** – Good most of the time

- **Daylight** – Warms up outdoor scenes

- **Cloudy** – Adds warmth to overcast shots (great for portraits)

- **Tungsten** – Cools down orange indoor light

- **Fluorescent** – Compensates for greenish overhead lights

- **Custom** – Manually set based on a white or gray object in the scene

Fix orange photos indoors? Try setting White Balance to Tungsten. Shooting under trees or in shade? Use Cloudy to warm it up.

To adjust White Balance:

Menu > Shooting Tab > White Balance

You can even fine-tune white balance manually by shifting the color toward blue, red, green, or amber.

Using Creative Filters Without Editing Software

The Canon R100 includes Creative Filters you can apply *before* or *after* shooting in JPEG mode. Think of these like Instagram filters, but built right into your camera—no app required.

Here are some options:

- **Grainy B/W** – Gritty, high-contrast black-and-white

- **Soft Focus** – Adds a dreamy, glowing blur

- **Fish-Eye Effect** – Warps the image for playful drama

- **Miniature Effect** – Blurs top and bottom, making scenes look like tiny models

- **Toy Camera** – Adds vignetting and shifts color for vintage style

To access Creative Filters:

Set the Mode Dial to Scene (SCN) > Choose Creative Filter

Or in Playback Mode, select an image > Choose "Creative Filters" from the Q Menu

Tip: Filters only apply to JPEGs, not RAW files. So if you're shooting RAW, they won't show unless you process them in-camera.

In-Camera RAW vs. JPEG: Which to Use and When

Let's talk file types. This decision shapes how much control you have later—and how easy your workflow is now.

JPEG

- Smaller file size
- Ready to share, print, or upload

- Applies Picture Style, White Balance, and noise reduction in-camera

- Limited editing flexibility later

Use when:

You want fast results, plan to apply Picture Styles in-camera, and don't want to edit afterward.

RAW

- Larger files, unprocessed

- Preserves every detail

- Requires post-processing (like in Lightroom)

- More flexibility to fix mistakes or change style later

Use when:

You want maximum image quality, plan to edit your photos, or need flexibility for professional work.

On the R100, you can shoot:

- RAW only

- JPEG only

- Or RAW + JPEG (best of both worlds)

If you're just starting out: Shoot in JPEG first.

When you're ready to explore editing, switch to RAW.

Final Thoughts: The Look You Want Is Already Inside Your Camera

You don't need expensive software to create stunning photos.

You already have creative tools built into your Canon R100 that let you shape the mood, emotion, and color of every shot. The key is to experiment:

- Try Portrait Picture Style with Cloudy White Balance at golden hour.

- Shoot a black-and-white street scene in Monochrome.

- Use Toy Camera Filter at a vintage market for a nostalgic vibe.

- Fine-tune Standard Picture Style with +2 saturation for a vibrant travel photo.

- Or try RAW + JPEG, so you always have options.

You are the artist. The R100 is your brush.

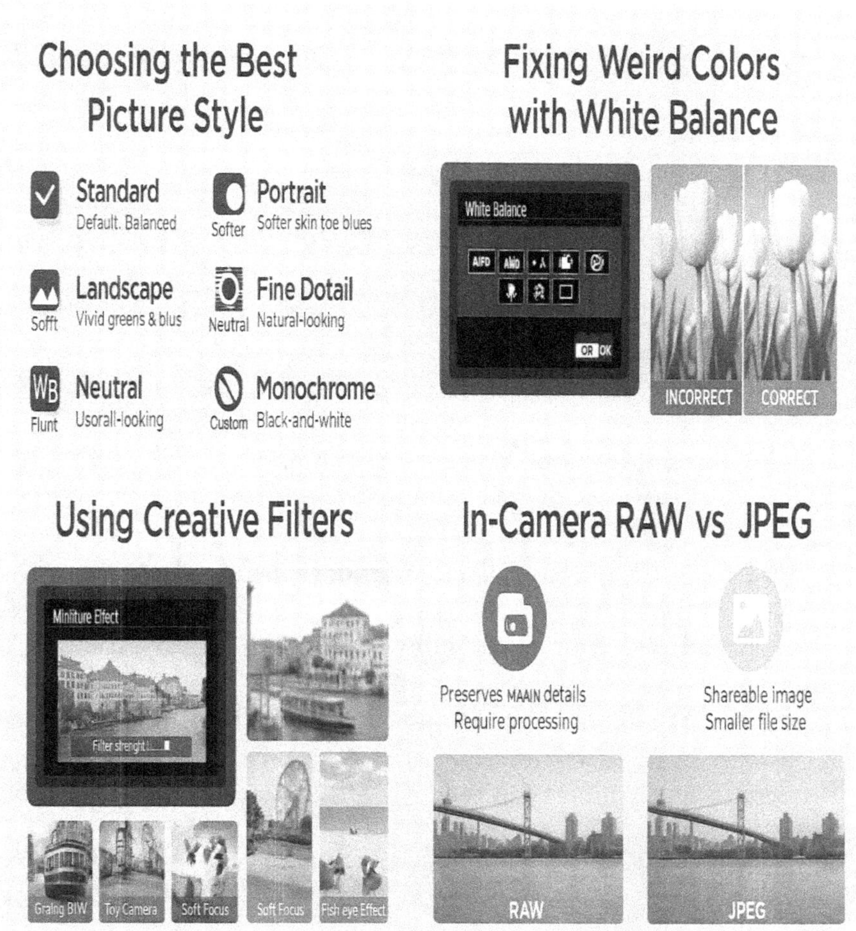

Chapter 7

Shooting Beautiful Videos with the Canon R100

Video is where memories move. Let's make sure yours look and sound amazing.

Photography captures moments. Video tells stories. And with the Canon EOS R100, you're holding a camera capable of telling yours beautifully—whether it's a toddler's first steps, a travel diary, or a quick tutorial for your YouTube channel.

But here's the honest truth: if you've tried shooting video with your R100 and ended up with shaky, blurry, or weirdly focused clips, you're not alone. Most people hit a wall the first few tries—not because the camera isn't capable, but because video requires a slightly different mindset (and setup) than stills.

In this chapter, we'll walk you through everything you need to shoot clean, clear, professional-looking video. No overwhelm. No jargon. Just real-world advice that works.

Quick Start Guide to Recording Video

Let's start with the basics—how to actually shoot a video with your Canon EOS R100.

1. Turn the Mode Dial to the Movie Camera icon (Movie mode).

2. Use the Menu to select video quality settings (more on that soon).

3. Frame your subject using the LCD screen (you can't use the viewfinder in video mode).

4. Press the red record button near the shutter (or on-screen).

5. Press it again to stop.

That's it.

Important: The Canon R100 does **not** support 4K at 60fps or advanced frame rates. It shoots:

- Full HD (1920 x 1080) at 24p, 30p, and 60p

- 4K at 24p (but with a crop and no Dual Pixel AF—explained below)

For most users, Full HD 1080p at 30fps is the perfect starting point.

Solving "Why Does My Video Look Blurry or Jerky?"

This is one of the most common complaints—and the easiest to fix once you know what's going on.

Here are the top causes and their quick solutions:

1. Shutter Speed Too Slow or Too Fast

- For natural motion, your shutter speed should be double your frame rate.

o   Shooting at 30fps? Use 1/60s shutter speed.

o   Shooting at 60fps? Use 1/125s.

Fix: Set your camera to Manual video mode and adjust shutter speed manually.

2. Autofocus is "hunting" during the clip

- If your camera keeps refocusing while recording, it creates that annoying "in and out" look.

Fix:

- Use Face + Eye Tracking if filming people.

- Tap to focus and then disable continuous AF for static subjects.

- Avoid using 4K on the R100 if you need smooth autofocus— it lacks Dual Pixel AF in 4K, making it prone to focus hunting.

3. Low Light = Grainy Footage

- Just like in still photography, higher ISO in video adds digital noise.

Fix:

- Use well-lit areas, even natural window light.
- Try f/2.8–f/4 aperture, ISO 400–800, and shutter 1/60s indoors.

4. Camera Movement is Unstable

- The Canon R100 doesn't have in-body stabilization.

Fix:

- Use a tripod, gimbal, or table support.
- Shoot with a lens that has Image Stabilization (IS) if handheld.
- Walk slowly, stabilize with elbows, or use a smartphone-style grip.

Video Autofocus Tricks

The Canon R100 has Dual Pixel Autofocus (DPAF) in Full HD video—which is excellent for tracking faces and maintaining smooth focus transitions.

Here's how to get the best from it:

Best Focus Settings for Video:

- **AF Method:** Face + Tracking

  Tracks faces and adjusts focus automatically.

- **AF Operation:** Movie Servo AF

  Enables continuous focus during recording.

- **Touch to Focus:** Tap the subject on the LCD screen to tell the camera where to lock in.

Pro Tip: If focus "jumps" during a take, tap on the background and then tap back on your subject. This resets the tracking without stopping the recording.

Best Settings for YouTube, Travel, and Family Videos

Let's match your settings to real-life goals.

For YouTube Videos (talking head, tutorials, sit-downs):

- **Resolution:** Full HD 1080p

- **Frame rate:** 30fps or 24fps (for cinematic look)

- **AF:** Face + Tracking + Movie Servo ON

- **Lens:** 18–45mm kit lens at 24–35mm works well

- **Shutter Speed:** 1/60s

- **Aperture:** f/2.8–f/4 for depth

- **Audio:** External mic (more below)

For Travel Clips (vlogs, scenery, daily footage):

- **Resolution:** 1080p at 60fps (smooth motion)

- **AF:** Servo with Face Tracking

- **Lens:** Wide-angle for walking shots (use Image Stabilization)

- **Shutter Speed:** 1/125s

- **ISO:** Auto ISO works fine here

For Family Moments (birthdays, playtime, events):

- **Resolution:** 1080p at 30fps

- **AF:** Servo ON with Face Tracking

- **Lens:** Whatever's convenient—kit lens works great

- **Stabilization:** Use a mini tripod or hold steady

Do not record important footage in 4K unless you're okay with no autofocus. For most people, 1080p is safer and better looking.

Audio Input Options and Limitations

Here's where many video beginners trip up: bad audio ruins great video.

Your Canon R100 has a built-in microphone, but like most DSLRs and mirrorless cameras, it picks up:

- Wind

- Echo

- Handling noise (your fingers, the strap)

To improve your audio:

- Use an external microphone—the R100 has a 3.5mm mic input jack.

- Plug in a Rode VideoMicro, Deity D4 Duo, or similar on-camera mic.

- For interviews or voiceovers, consider a lavalier mic clipped to the speaker's shirt.

Audio Tips:

- Test levels before filming (no peaking into the red).

- Avoid noisy environments.

- Don't rely solely on built-in mics for important moments.

Note: The Canon R100 has no headphone jack—so you can't monitor audio in real time. Always do a quick playback test.

Memory Card Limits & Overheating Warnings

Memory Card for Video

Shooting video requires fast, reliable cards. Here's what to use:

- UHS-I, Class 10 or V30 rated SD card
- Minimum 32GB (for casual use), 64–128GB for longer sessions

Recording time per 64GB (approx):

- 1080p at 30fps: ~2 hours
- 4K at 24fps: ~1 hour (but cropped + limited focus)

Overheating Warnings

The Canon R100 is not a professional cinema camera. It can overheat during long 4K sessions or in hot environments.

Tips to avoid overheating:

- Record in 1080p, especially indoors.

- Break up longer recordings into smaller clips (under 20 minutes).

- Let the camera rest if it feels hot.

1080p recording is very stable. Stick with it for everyday use—it's easier, smoother, and less risky.

Final Thoughts: Video That Captures the Moment Beautifully

You don't need to be a filmmaker to shoot beautiful videos. But you *do* need to understand how your camera sees motion, light, and sound.

The Canon EOS R100 makes this accessible—especially in Full HD. Start small. Practice framing. Learn what good audio sounds like. Use your camera like a creative partner, not just a recorder.

- For home moments: prioritize stability and focus

- For YouTube: control your audio and lighting

- For memories in motion: let Face Tracking do the heavy lifting

SHOOTING BEAUTIFUL VIDEOS WITH THE CANON R100

QUICK START GUIDE TO RECORDING VIDEO

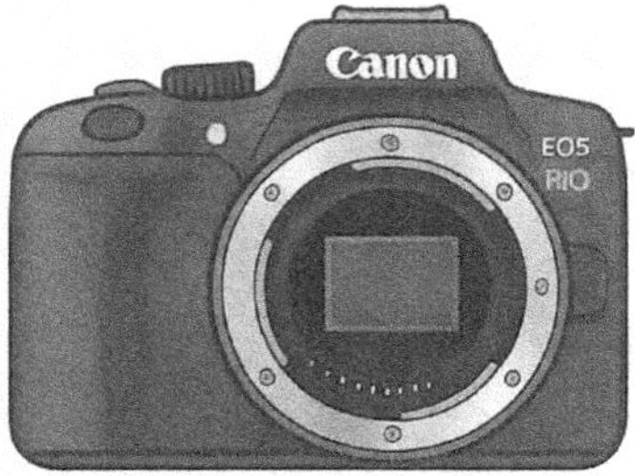

SET TO MOVIE MODE

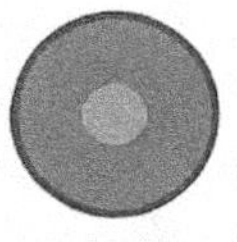
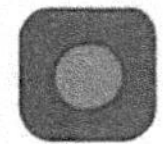

PRESS TO RECORD

Solving "Why Does My Video Look Blurry or Jerky?"

Shutter speed wrong
for frame rate

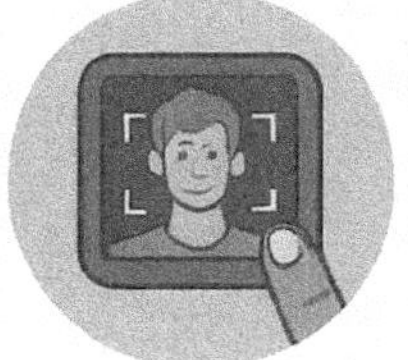

Autofocus is shifting
during recording

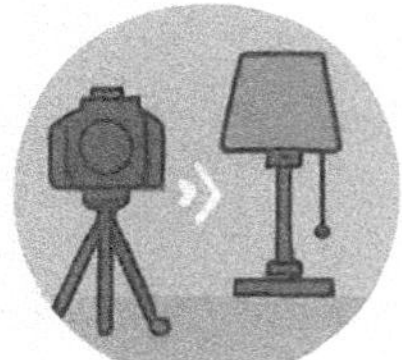

Clip is too dark
or video is grainy

Video Autofocus Tricks

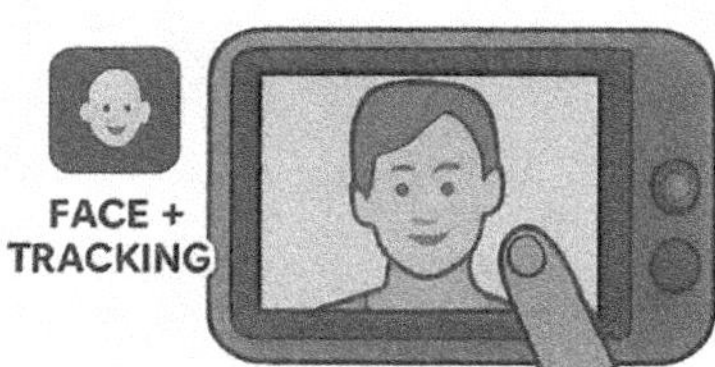

Touch screen to focus

Audio Input Options and Limitations

Best Settings for YouTube, Travel, and Family Videos

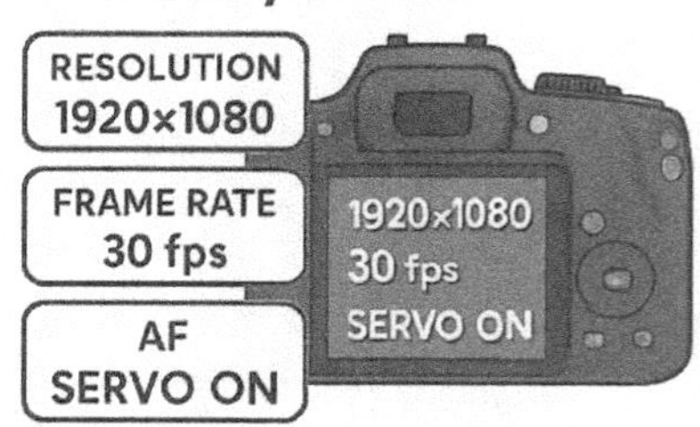

BEST SETTINGS 3) LIMITATIONS

Chapter 8

Connecting, Sharing & Transferring Photos

Because what's the point of a great photo if it's stuck in your camera?

You've captured the perfect moment. The lighting was right. The expression was real. You're ready to share it—maybe with your family, your Instagram followers, or just to back it up before it's forgotten.

And then it hits: the tech struggle.

Bluetooth won't connect. Wi-Fi keeps dropping. The Canon app spins forever. Maybe your camera doesn't show up at all.

Take a breath.

This chapter is your shortcut through all that. You'll learn—clearly and calmly—how to connect your Canon R100 to your phone, tablet, or computer, how to transfer photos reliably, and how to troubleshoot when things go sideways.

You'll finally feel like your camera isn't just capturing memories, but *sharing* them—easily.

How to Use the Canon Camera Connect App

Let's start with Canon's official mobile app: Canon Camera Connect. It's free, and it's your gateway to transferring photos wirelessly and even controlling the camera remotely.

What You Can Do With the App:

- View photos on your camera *from your phone*

- Transfer full-res or downsized images/videos to your device

- Geotag your photos

- Remotely control the camera for self-portraits or tripod shots

Getting Set Up (First-Time Only)

1. **Download the App:**

Search "Canon Camera Connect" in the App Store (iOS) or Google Play (Android).

2. **Enable Wi-Fi on Your Camera:**

   o Go to Menu > Function Settings > Wireless communication settings

   o Enable Wi-Fi/NFC and Bluetooth

3. **Pair Your Phone via Bluetooth:**

   o In the app, select your camera model.

   o Follow prompts to pair via Bluetooth first—it's more stable.

   o Once paired, you'll be able to establish a Wi-Fi connection when needed.

4. **Establish Wi-Fi Connection:**

   o The app will prompt you to switch to the camera's Wi-Fi network.

- o Your phone will show a Canon Wi-Fi signal—connect to it.

Once connected, you can browse, select, and transfer your photos wirelessly.

Tip: The first connection can feel clunky. Once it's paired, future transfers are much quicker.

Bluetooth vs. Wi-Fi: What's Better and Why

These two are both used for camera communication, but they serve different purposes.

Bluetooth:

- Low-power, always-on connection

- Enables auto connection

- Used to start/control Wi-Fi transfers

- Limited for actual file transfers

Best for: Quick pairing, GPS tagging, background control

Wi-Fi:

- High-speed connection

- Used for transferring photos and videos

- Needed for live view remote control

Best for: Image transfer, remote shooting

How it works:

Bluetooth gets you connected easily. Wi-Fi does the heavy lifting.

Use both together for a smoother experience.

Transferring Photos to Phone, Tablet, or PC

To a Smartphone or Tablet:

- Open Canon Camera Connect

- Tap Images on camera

- Select photos > Download

- Choose original or reduced size

To a Computer (No Cables Needed):

Wi-Fi Transfer (PC/Mac):

1. Download EOS Utility Software from Canon's website

2. Enable Wi-Fi/NFC on the camera

3. On your computer, connect to the R100's Wi-Fi

4. Use EOS Utility to transfer files or shoot tethered

Via USB Cable (Reliable & Fast):

1. Turn off the camera

2. Plug in using a USB-C cable (or USB-A depending on your setup)

3. Camera will appear as a drive, or launch Image Capture (Mac) or EOS Utility (Windows)

4. Drag-and-drop or import as needed

USB is still the fastest and most reliable method for large file batches.

Direct Print Options & Cloud Backup

Want to print without detouring through a computer?

Print Directly to Wireless Printer:

- Make sure your printer supports PictBridge over Wi-Fi

- On the camera, go to Menu > Print Settings

- Connect directly to your printer's Wi-Fi

- Select and print photos from the camera

Cloud Backup with Canon Image Gateway (Optional):

Canon offers Image.Canon, a cloud storage service that syncs your media online.

- Requires a Canon ID (free to create)

- Uploads JPEGs, RAWs, and videos

- Limited storage (free tier has a cap)

- Allows auto-transfer from camera to cloud via Wi-Fi

Better options for cloud backup:

- Google Photos (for JPEGs from your phone)

- Dropbox, OneDrive, or iCloud Drive (manually transfer via phone/computer)

Solving Connection Errors and App Not Working

Here's the part most guides don't help with—but we will. Because yes, sometimes it just doesn't work.

Problem: Camera not showing in app

Fix:

- Ensure camera's Bluetooth and Wi-Fi are both on

- Make sure no other phone is already connected

- Restart both devices

- Forget and re-pair in your phone's Bluetooth settings

Problem: App stuck on "Connecting" or won't transfer files

Fix:

- Toggle Wi-Fi OFF/ON on your camera

- Force-close and restart the Canon app

- Reconnect to the correct camera Wi-Fi network

- Try again with the camera in Playback mode

Problem: Images not appearing in app

Fix:

- Use the "Images on camera" tab, not Live View

- Ensure you're not in 4K recording mode (some files may not preview)

- Try selecting only JPEGs (RAWs may be unsupported for viewing)

General Troubleshooting Tips:

- Keep the camera firmware up to date (via Canon's site)

- Turn off battery-saving modes during connection

- Use a fresh battery during transfers (Wi-Fi drains power)

Worst case? Use a memory card reader or USB cable to transfer manually. Old-school, but 100% reliable.

Final Thoughts: Your Photos Deserve to Be Seen

A camera isn't just a tool to capture what matters. It's a bridge between you and the people you love, the stories you share, the world you want to remember. But if your photos stay trapped inside a memory card, you miss half the magic.

The Canon R100 has everything you need to stay connected—but technology sometimes forgets to keep it simple. Now that you know how to pair, share, transfer, and troubleshoot, you'll never again say,

"I took a great photo... but I can't get it off my camera."

CONNECTING, SHARING ARING & TRANSFERRING PHOTOS

HOW TO USE THE CANON CAMERA CONNECT APP

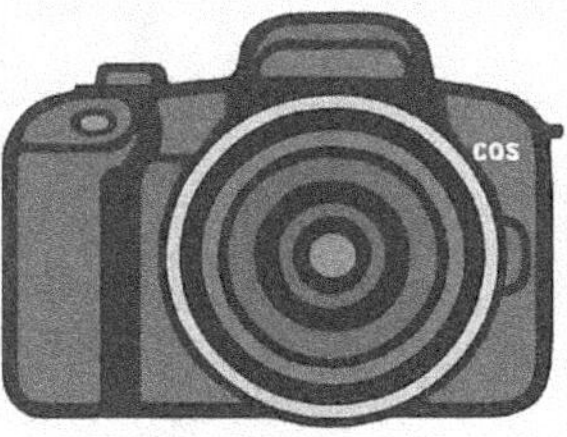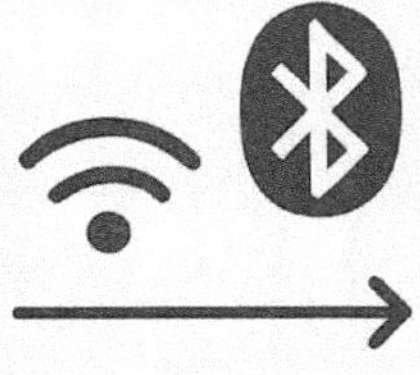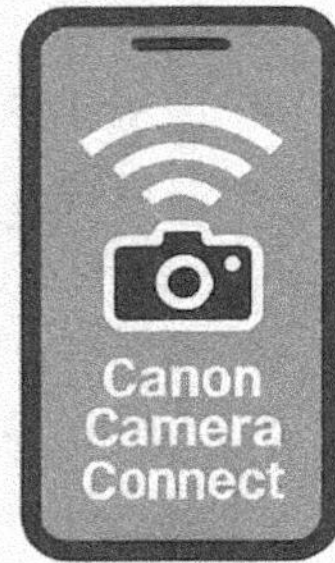

- **Download the Canon Camera Connect app** to your phone or tablet
- **On the camera:** Enable Wi-Fi in the menu
- **Pair the camera with phone** via Bluetooth

Faster transfer
Remote shooting
Needed for full control

TRANSFERRING PHOTOS TO PHONE, TABLET, OR PC

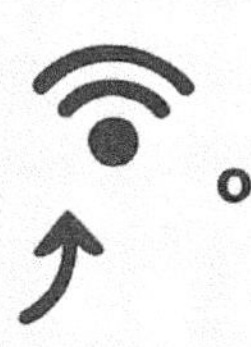
or
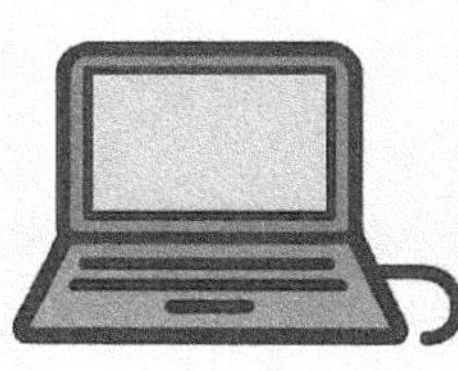

Select photos in the app and tap the import icon

Connect camera to PC with the USB cable

Also works with certain wireless printers

SOLVING CONNECTION ERRORS AND APP NOT WORKING

- Enable Wi-Fi on phone and camera
- Test Bluetooth pairing again
- Restart the camera and app

- Test Bluetooth pairing again
- Confirm the camera is in playback mode

Chapter 9

Troubleshooting Common Problems

Because even the best camera can act up. Here's how to stay calm and fix it fast.

You picked up your Canon EOS R100 to create—not to stress over error messages, blinking lights, or unresponsive buttons. But even the best gear has its hiccups. When things go wrong, it's easy to panic or feel like you broke something. You didn't.

Cameras are like tiny computers with lenses—they can freeze, crash, or misbehave just like your phone or laptop. The good news? Most problems have simple fixes once you know where to look.

This chapter is your troubleshooting safety net. We'll walk through the most common real-world issues R100 users face and—step by step—show you how to solve them without guesswork or tech jargon.

Memory Card Errors (and Recovery Tips)

A dreaded "Card Cannot Be Accessed" message is enough to ruin your day—especially if you've just taken great photos. But stay calm.

Here's what to do:

Step-by-Step Fix:

1. **Remove and Reinsert the Card**

   o   Power off the camera.

   o   Gently remove the SD card, wait 10 seconds, reinsert, and power on.

   o   Sometimes it's just a bad connection.

2. **Try Another Card**

o If the message persists, try a second SD card (preferably one you know works).

o If the camera reads it, the issue is likely the card—not the camera.

3. **Format the Card in the Camera**

   o WARNING: This **deletes all content** on the card.

   o Go to Menu → Setup Tab → Format Card

   o If the card formats and works again, you're good to go.

4. **Use a Computer to Recover Photos (If Needed)**

   o If the card contains photos you can't lose, don't reformat.

   o Instead, use recovery software like Recuva (PC) or Disk Drill (Mac) to attempt retrieval.

Prevention Tips:

• Always format a new SD card in your camera, not your computer.

- Use UHS-I, Class 10 SD cards (Canon-approved specs).

- Avoid removing the card while the camera is still powered on.

- Don't delete photos mid-shoot; wait until transfer to manage files.

Camera Freezes, Lag, or Won't Turn On

This can feel scary—like your camera died. It almost never has.

Try This First:

1. **Remove the Battery**

   o Turn off the camera.

   o Take the battery out for 15–30 seconds.

   o Reinsert and power on.

2. **Check the Battery Charge**

   o A nearly dead battery can cause freezing or failure to boot.

   o Try a full recharge or swap in a fresh battery.

3. **Take Out the SD Card**

   o A corrupted or incompatible card can crash the system.

   o Try starting the camera with the card removed.

4. **Reset to Factory Defaults**

   o If the issue continues, reset the camera (instructions below).

Still no power?

- Try a different battery and charger.

- If still unresponsive, contact Canon support—it could be hardware-related.

Autofocus Not Working? Do This.

It's frustrating when you press the shutter halfway—and nothing happens.

Checklist:

1. **Is the lens switched to AF (not MF)?**

   o   Some lenses have a manual/auto switch. Set it to AF.

2. **Check the AF Method in Menu**

   o   Go to Menu → AF Tab → AF Method

   o   Choose Face + Tracking **or** 1-point AF for more control.

3. **Low Light? Add Light**

   o   Autofocus struggles in dark conditions.

   o   Try shooting with more ambient light or use the camera's AF-assist beam.

4. **Lens Not Properly Attached**

   o   Remove and reattach the lens.

   o   Ensure it clicks into place securely.

Tip: The camera won't autofocus in Manual (M) Focus mode— check your mode dial and AF settings.

Battery Drains Too Fast? Check These Settings.

Your battery should last for several hundred shots or hours of standby—but some settings quietly chew through power.

Battery-Saving Checklist:

1. **Turn Off Wi-Fi/Bluetooth When Not Needed**

   o Menu → Setup → Wireless Settings → Disable both

2. **Lower LCD Screen Brightness**

   o Menu → Display settings → LCD Brightness

3. **Shorten Auto Power-Off Time**

   o Set it to 1 minute or less to save power when not in use.

4. **Avoid Excessive Image Review**

   o Constantly checking your photos burns battery faster than shooting.

5. **Use Eco Mode**

o   Menu → Display → Eco Mode ON

6. **Turn Off Continuous AF (When Not Needed)**

   o   This feature constantly hunts focus, even when idle.

Tip: Carry a second battery if you plan to shoot all day, especially with video.

Lens Not Detected or Won't Zoom?

You turn on your R100, and it says "Lens Not Attached." Or maybe your zoom doesn't work. Let's fix that.

Lens Connection Fix:

1. Power off the camera

2. Remove the lens

3. Check the gold contacts on both camera and lens—are they clean?

   o   Wipe gently with a microfiber cloth if dirty

4. Reattach the lens firmly until you hear the click

5. Turn the camera on and try again

Some beginner users forget: Canon's kit lens (18–45mm) must be manually unlocked before use.

Twist the zoom ring until it clicks out to extend.

Bonus: Zoom Not Working?

- The kit lens is mechanical, not motorized.

- You must twist the barrel to zoom manually—no buttons or switches will do it.

Resetting Camera to Factory Defaults

Sometimes, you just need a fresh start. Whether your settings are scrambled or you want to clear everything and begin again, a reset can work wonders.

How to Reset:

1. Go to Menu

2. Navigate to Setup Tab

3. Scroll to Clear Settings

4. Choose:

  o Clear all camera settings (restores default shooting
    functions)

  o Clear all Custom Functions (removes user-defined
    customizations)

This does not delete photos or format your SD card—it only resets camera behavior.

Final Thoughts: Don't Panic, Just Reset and Reboot

The truth is, tech glitches are a part of digital photography. It doesn't mean you've failed. It means your gear is complex—and every system sometimes needs a nudge.

Whenever something feels broken:

- Breathe.

- Turn it off.

- Reboot.

- Reseat the lens, the battery, or the card.

- Double-check your settings.

And know this: you're not alone. Every professional photographer has faced camera hiccups in the middle of a shoot. The difference is—they've learned to troubleshoot calmly.

Now, so have you.

MEMORY CARD ERRORS

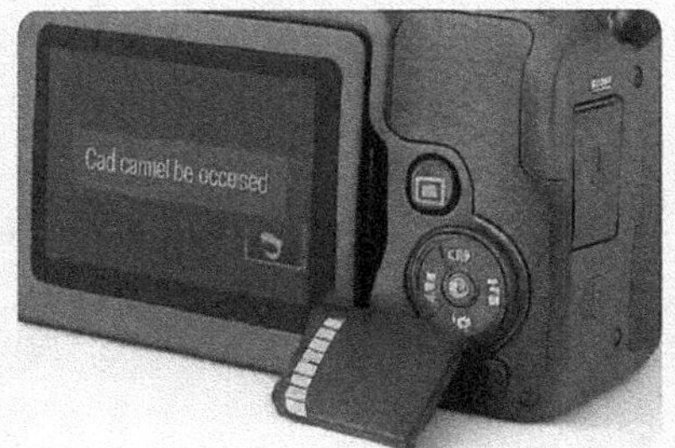

- Remove and reinsert the card
- Try another memory card
- Format card in camera if possible
- Use recovery software if needed

CAMERA FREEZES, LAG, OR WON'T ON

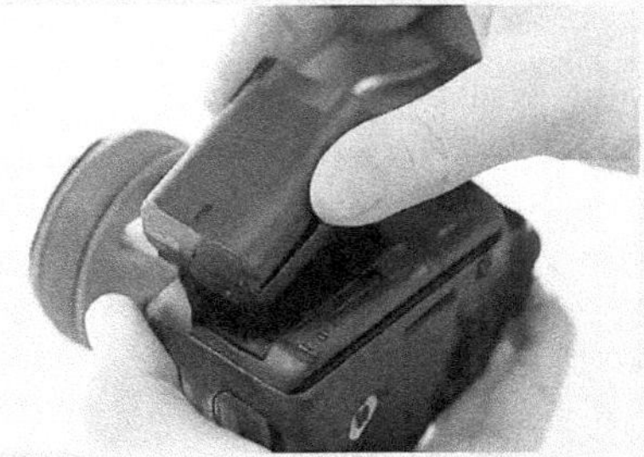

- Remove the battery, then rersert
- Check battery charge level
- Take out and reinsert memoy.card
- Reset camera to factory settings

AUTOFOCUS NOT WORKING?

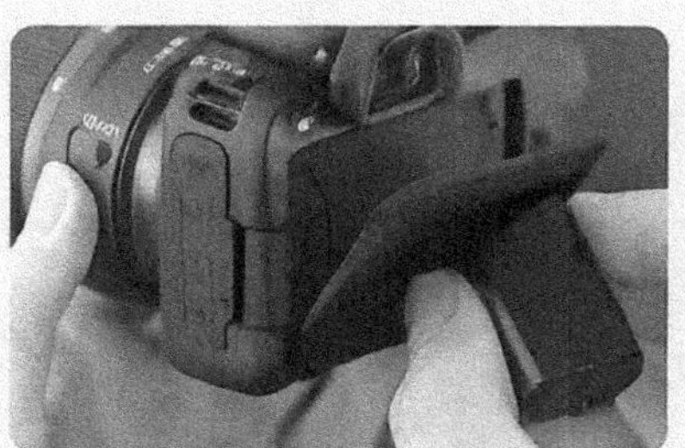

- Check that lens is in AF mode
- Update AF mode in menu
- Ensure adequate lighting
- Clean the lens & contacts

RESETTING CAMERA TO FACTORY DEFAULTS

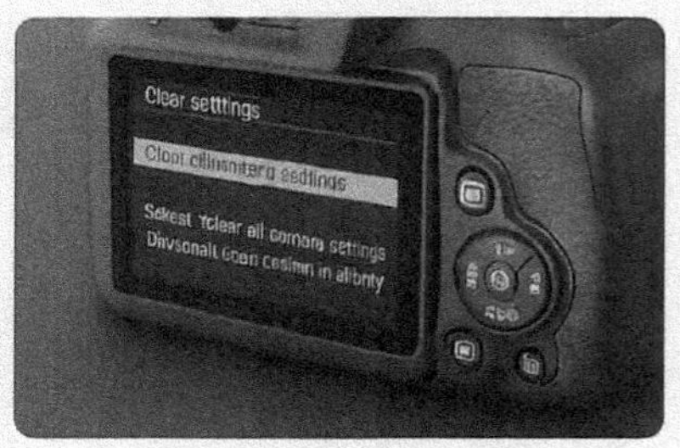

- In the menu, go to "Clear settings"
- Select "Clear all camera settings"
- Optional: reset custom functions

BATTERY DRAINS TOO FAST?

- Turn off Wi-Fi and Bluetooth
- Lower the LCD brightness
- Use the camera's Eco mode

Chapter 10

Tips for Better Everyday Photos

Because life happens fast—and your photos should feel like it.

There's a kind of beauty in everyday moments that doesn't ask for permission. It's in your child's unguarded giggle, your partner's sleepy morning face, your dog mid-jump, or the golden hush just before sunset. But sometimes when you try to capture it... something's missing.

Maybe the photo is too dark. Maybe the focus missed. Maybe it just didn't feel like it did when you saw it with your own eyes.

The good news? The Canon EOS R100 is more than capable of catching magic. You just need a little guidance—and that's exactly what this chapter is for.

You'll learn real-world camera settings and small tricks that make a *big* difference, even if you're not a pro. Let's make sure you never miss a moment that matters again.

Best R100 Settings for Portraits

People are not just subjects—they're stories. And the R100 is fantastic at telling them, if you let it.

Your Go-To Portrait Settings:

- **Mode Dial:** Aperture Priority (**Av**)

- **Aperture (f/stop):** Set to **f/2.8 to f/5.6** for soft, blurred backgrounds

- **Lens Tip:** Use the kit lens at 45mm or upgrade to a 50mm f/1.8 for dreamy portraits

- **Focus Mode: Face + Tracking AF**

- **Drive Mode: One-shot** for still portraits, **Servo AF** for kids or moving subjects

- **White Balance:** Auto or adjust for warmth if indoors

- **ISO:** Auto (capped at 1600)

Try photographing your subject near a window with soft natural light. You'll get beautifully lit skin tones without harsh shadows.

Travel Photography Tips (with Light Gear)

When you're on the road, you don't want to be fiddling with a thousand settings or carrying too much. But you still want the shot.

Travel Settings to Use:

- **Mode Dial:** Scene Intelligent Auto or Program (**P**) if you're in a hurry

- **Aperture Priority (Av):** for cityscapes, street shots, and depth control

- **AF Mode:** Face + Tracking or Zone AF for people on the move

- **Drive Mode: High-speed continuous** for capturing fleeting moments

- **White Balance:** Daylight or Cloudy for vibrant travel color

- **Image Quality: RAW + JPEG** if you want editing flexibility later

- **Lens Advice:** Stick to the kit lens or add a compact zoom (like a 55-210mm) for versatility

Bonus: Keep a microfiber cloth in your bag. Dust, humidity, or smudges can ruin a perfect travel photo.

Indoor & Low Light Tricks Without Flash

Flash can flatten everything—especially emotion. Luckily, you can shoot beautifully in low light without ever popping that harsh front light.

Try This Setup:

- **Mode Dial: Av** (Aperture Priority)

- **Aperture:** As wide as possible (f/2.8 or lower)

- **ISO:** Increase to 1600 or 3200 if needed

- **Shutter Speed:** Try to keep it 1/60 sec or faster for handheld shots

- **White Balance:** Tungsten or Auto (then warm it up slightly in post if needed)

- **Use a Stable Surface:** A table, shelf, or even your elbow on a chair can act like a tripod

Light a candle, turn on a lamp, or pull open the curtain. Low light doesn't mean no light—it just needs to be thoughtful.

Capturing Kids and Pets in Motion

Fast. Unpredictable. Adorable. That's the trifecta of shooting little humans and furballs. And yes, it *can* be done beautifully with the R100.

Here's What to Use:

- **Mode Dial:** Shutter Priority (Tv)

- **Shutter Speed:** Start at 1/500s or faster

- **AF Mode:** Servo AF (Continuous focus)

- **Drive Mode:** High-speed continuous

- **ISO:** Auto (let the camera help with exposure)

- **Focus Points:** Use Zone AF to keep the subject within the zone

- **Lens Tip:** Zoom in and shoot from a distance—they act more natural when they don't know they're being photographed

Tip: Don't wait for the "perfect" moment. Shoot in bursts—you'll often find gold in the in-between frames.

Taking Better Selfies or Group Photos

Whether it's a solo adventure or a family BBQ, you want to be *in* the memories, not just behind the camera.

Your Selfie/Group Setup:

- **Mode Dial:** Scene Intelligent Auto

- **Lens:** Use a wider focal length (18mm–24mm)

- **Timer:** Set to 10 sec with Continuous Shots = 3

- **Focus Mode:** Face + Tracking

- **Stabilize:** Use a mini tripod or stable surface

- **Remote Trigger:** Use the Canon Camera Connect app as a remote shutter release

Pro trick: You can compose your group shot from your phone using the app's live view feature. No guessing.

Using Burst Mode and Timers Creatively

These two are often overlooked, but they're small tools that unlock big creative potential.

Burst Mode Ideas:

- Capture a child jumping into a pool

- Document the stages of a genuine laugh

- Get the exact moment your pet leaps for a toy

- Freeze movement in street photography

Set your Drive Mode to High-Speed Continuous, then hold the shutter as the action unfolds.

Timer Ideas:

- Solo long exposures at night (with no hand shake)

- Street scenes where you want to blend into the background

- Self-portraits with dramatic lighting

- Creative time-lapse sequences

Think of the timer and burst not just as functions—but as creative companions.

Final Thoughts: Emotion Over Perfection

The most beautiful photos aren't always technically perfect. They don't always follow the "rules." But they feel *alive*. They tell the truth of the moment.

Use the R100 not just to document your life, but to celebrate it. These settings and tips aren't about complexity—they're about removing barriers so your real, everyday world can shine through in your images.

Let the light be imperfect. Let the smiles be messy. Let the background be what it is.

Just shoot. Often. Bravely. With care.

Because five years from now, when you look back, you won't care if the ISO was 400 or 1600. You'll care that you caught the feeling.

TIPS FOR BETTER EVERYDAY PHOTOS

BEST SETTINGS FOR PORTRATS

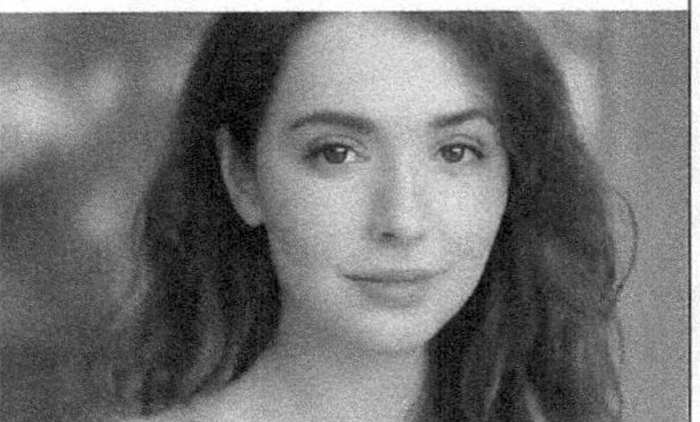

- Mode: Av (aperture priority
- Aperture: f/2.8
- Focus: face tracking

TRAVEL PHOTOGRAPHY TIPS

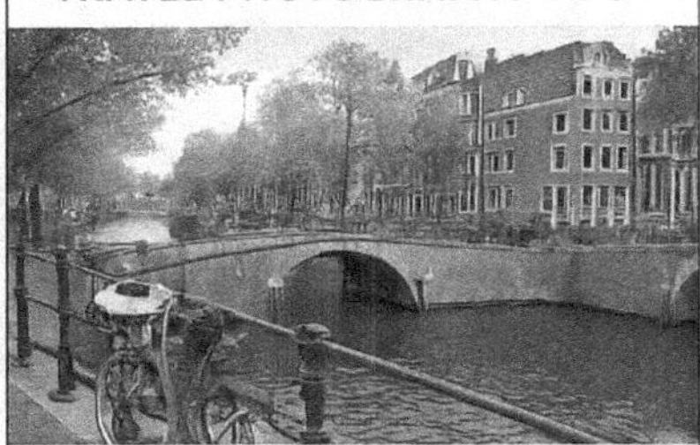

- Light gear only
- Drive mode: continuous

INDOOR & LOW LIGHT WITHOUT FLASH

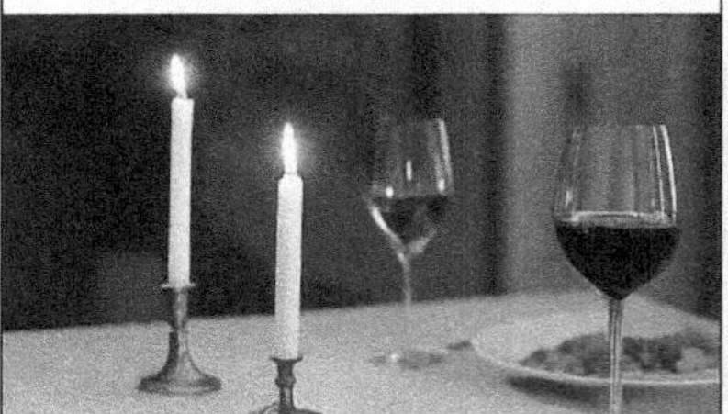

- Mode: Av
- ISO: 1600 or higher

CAPTURING KIDS AND PETS IN MOTION

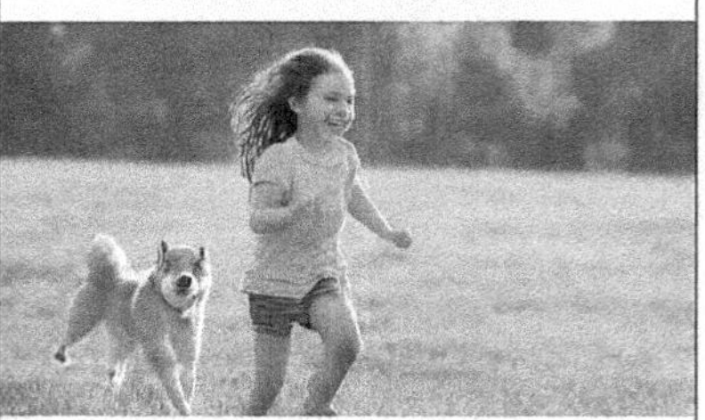

- Mode: Ty
- Shutter speed: 1/500 s or faster

BETTER SELFIES OR GROUP PHOTOS

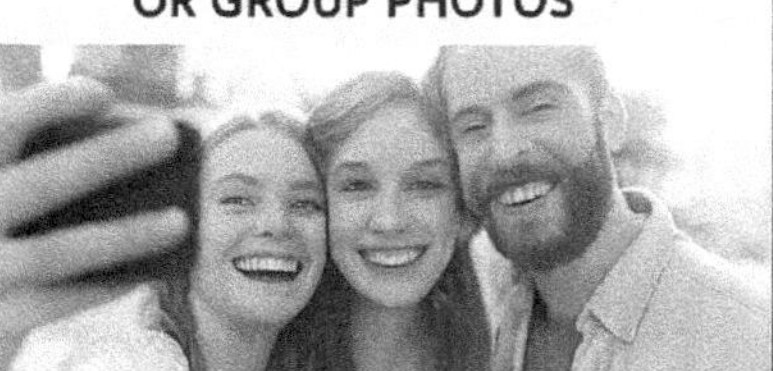

- Timer: 10 sec . delay

USING BURST MODE AND TIMERS

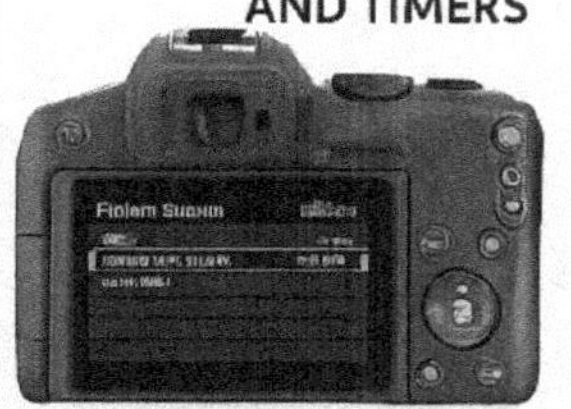

- Burst: capture fast action

Chapter 11

Editing Basics and Organizing Your Photos

Because a photo's story doesn't end when you click the shutter—it begins there.

You've just spent the day capturing your child's birthday, the way sunlight poured through your kitchen window, or a once-in-a-lifetime vacation moment. You've got the shots. But now what?

This chapter is for the after—the *what now?* stage that so many beginners fear. You're not alone if your camera roll feels like a digital junk drawer. You're also not alone if editing seems mysterious or intimidating.

The good news is: editing and organizing don't have to be complicated. With the right tools and simple systems, you'll gain

143

full control over your photos, preserve what matters, and turn everyday images into something you'll be proud to share, print, and keep forever.

Let's start from scratch and walk you through it—no jargon, no overwhelm. Just practical steps that make sense.

Free Editing Apps to Start With

You don't need expensive software to make your photos shine. Some of the most beginner-friendly and powerful editing tools are free—and available right on your phone or computer.

Best Free Apps (for Mobile):

- **Snapseed (iOS & Android)**

    o Easy, intuitive controls

    o Powerful "Tune Image," healing tool, and filters

    o Great for color correction and fixing lighting issues

- **Lightroom Mobile (Free Version)**

- o Advanced editing made simple

- o Presets and sliders for brightness, contrast, and more

- o You can upgrade later for desktop sync/cloud storage

- **Canva (Mobile/Desktop)**

  - o Fantastic for creating collages or adding text to images

  - o Beginner-friendly for social media-style edits

Start simple: brighten shadows, reduce highlights, and bump contrast slightly. Small changes often make a big difference.

How to Use Canon's Digital Photo Professional (DPP)

Canon provides its own free editing software—Digital Photo Professional (DPP)—which is especially helpful if you shoot RAW images with your EOS R100.

Getting Started:

1. **Download it from Canon's website**

   o   Look for the version that matches your camera model and operating system

2. **Import your images**

   o   Plug in your camera or SD card

   o   Select the folder and choose the photos you want to edit

3. **Basic Workflow Inside DPP:**

   o   Adjust exposure, contrast, white balance

   o   Use the "Highlight/Shadow" sliders to rescue blown-out skies or dark corners

   o   Crop and straighten your image

   o   Save as JPEG when finished

Pros:

- Tailor-made for Canon color science

- Non-destructive RAW editing

- Totally free

Heads-Up:

- Slower than apps like Lightroom

- Clunky interface, but manageable with time

Organizing Your Photos Like a Pro (Tags, Dates, Folders)

A photo that's lost in a sea of "IMG_1234" filenames is a photo you may never see again. Let's fix that.

The "3-Click Rule":

You should be able to find any photo within 3 clicks or less.

Folder Structure That Works:

markdown

CopyEdit

/Photos

```
/2025

  /07-July

    /Family Picnic - July 5

    /Weekend Hike - July 12

  /08-August

    /Italy Trip - Rome
```

Tips:

- Name folders by event and date

- Inside each folder, separate by Camera RAW and Edited JPEGs

- Tag favorites using your software (Lightroom, Photos app, etc.)

- Use consistent naming like `2025-07-05_Picnic_001.jpg`

Remember: organization isn't just about tidiness. It's about rediscovering memories years later without frustration.

Backing Up Your Shots to Avoid Data Loss

Imagine this: your SD card gets corrupted or your laptop crashes. Hundreds of irreplaceable moments—gone in an instant. It's heartbreaking. And totally preventable.

Here's how to back up smartly:

1. Use a Physical Backup (External Hard Drive):

- After every major shoot or trip, copy files to an external drive

- Label drives by year and store safely

2. Use a Cloud Backup Service:

- Google Photos (15GB free, automatic sync)

- Dropbox or iCloud Drive

- Amazon Photos (unlimited if you're a Prime member)

Rule of Three: Keep your photos in three places—your computer, an external drive, and a cloud service.

Intro to Lightroom (If Upgrading Later)

When you're ready to go beyond the basics—or you're shooting more frequently—Adobe Lightroom is the gold standard for editing and organization.

What Lightroom Offers:

- Powerful non-destructive RAW editing

- Professional-grade color grading tools

- Presets for consistent editing styles

- Easy syncing between mobile and desktop

- Cataloging tools: tags, keywords, smart collections

Ideal Workflow in Lightroom:

1. Import and apply a preset or auto-enhance

2. Fine-tune exposure, contrast, and color

3. Tag photos by theme (e.g., Family, Travel, Pets)

4. Export or share directly

Lightroom isn't just editing software—it's your digital darkroom. If you grow in your photography, you'll grow into this.

Final Thoughts: From Chaos to Keepsake

Editing and organizing isn't just about tech. It's about preserving *meaning*—the story behind the image.

You don't need to master every tool overnight. Start by learning how to brighten a dark photo. Create your first folder labeled by date. Back up one precious image today, just in case.

These small steps turn scattered pixels into lasting memories. They give your photos structure, care, and a second life beyond the screen.

In the end, photography isn't only about capturing light. It's about keeping what matters close, and finding it again when you need it most.

FREE EDITING APPS TO START WITH

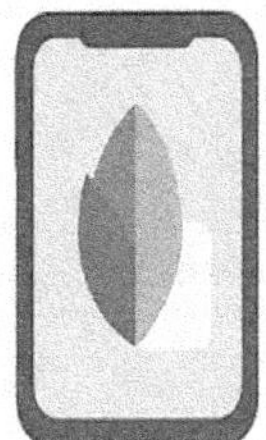

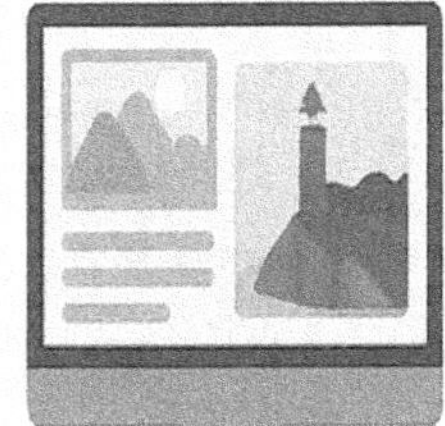

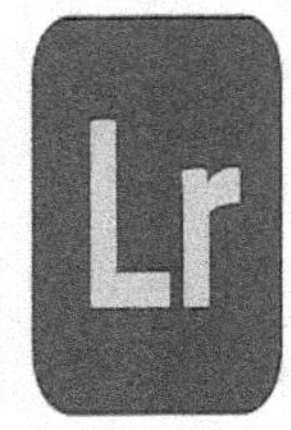

Snapseed

Simple tools for ajiusting or tweaking color

Canon DPP

Perfect for editing Canon RAW files

Lightroom

More advanced editing when you're ready

ORGANIZING YOUR PHOTOS

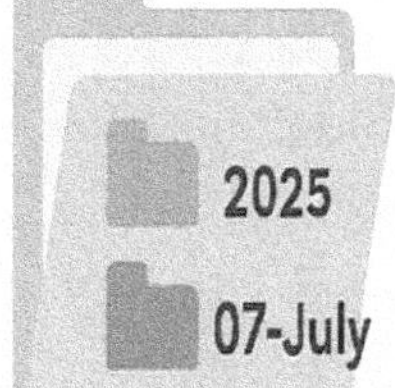

Create folders by date & event ★

Tag favorites

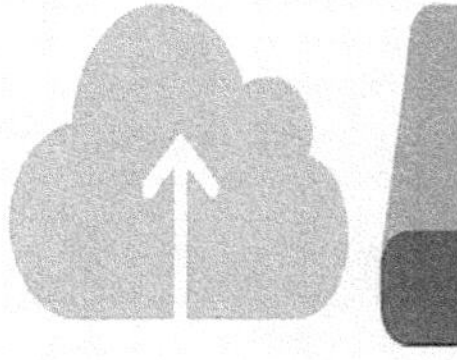

Back up to a cloud and external hard drive

INTRO TO LIGHTROOM

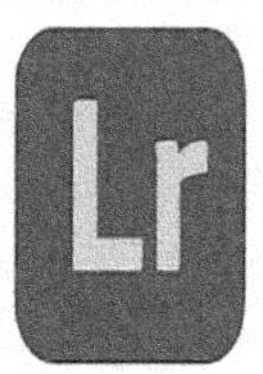

Powerful RAW editing and organizing

Chapter 12

Accessories That Actually Help (and Which to Skip)

Because you don't need everything—just the right things.

When you first get your Canon EOS R100, the temptation to buy *all the things* can be strong. Camera stores and online bundles can make you feel like you need every gadget, lens, or accessory under the sun to take decent photos.

But let's pause right there.

You don't need a drawer full of unused gear. What you *do* need are a few well-chosen tools that fit your style, simplify your shooting, and solve real-world problems.

This chapter is about cutting through the clutter. Whether you're buying your first tripod or wondering if that $200 filter is really worth it, you'll find clear, honest advice here to help you build your perfect starter kit—without overspending or falling for hype.

Let's break it down, piece by piece.

Must-Have Gear for Beginners

These are the accessories that *actually* make your Canon R100 experience better from day one.

1. Spare Battery

- The Canon R100 isn't known for having a marathon battery life, especially when shooting video.
- Get at least one extra LP-E17 battery.
- Keep it charged and ready in your camera bag.

Tip: Name your batteries with a sticker (e.g., BATT-1, BATT-2) so you always know which is freshly charged.

2. Fast SD Card (UHS-I, Class 10 or V30)

- Avoid slow cards—your camera will lag, and video may stop recording.

- Look for: SanDisk Extreme Pro, Lexar 1000x, or Sony Tough series.

- Recommended: 64GB–128GB, with read/write speeds of 90–170MB/s

3. Lightweight Tripod

- Perfect for low-light shots, family portraits, or YouTube-style videos.

- Look for tripods that are:
  - Compact & foldable (for travel or home)
  - Have a quick-release plate
  - Lightweight but stable (carbon fiber if budget allows)

Budget Pick: AmazonBasics or UBeesize

Midrange Pick: Manfrotto Compact Action

Premium Pick: Peak Design or Benro Slim

4. Camera Strap (Comfort > Fashion)

- The stock Canon strap can dig into your neck.

- Upgrade to a padded cross-body strap or a wrist strap for more casual use.

Brands to trust: Peak Design, BlackRapid, Altura

Tripods, Lenses, and Filters That Make a Difference

Kit Lens Add-On: Wide-Angle or Portrait Prime

While the R100's 18–45mm kit lens is a good starter, consider adding:

1. Canon RF 50mm f/1.8 STM ("Nifty Fifty")

- Crisp portraits with creamy background blur (bokeh)

- Great for indoor, food, and street photography

2. Canon RF 16mm f/2.8 STM

- Ideal for landscapes, interiors, vlogging, or group selfies

- Compact, wide, and very affordable

Filters (Only One You Really Need)

UV Filter

- Not for image quality—purely lens protection from scratches, dust, fingerprints

Optional:

- **Circular Polarizer**: Reduces reflections on water/glass and deepens sky blues

- **ND Filter**: For video shooters who want to keep shutter speed low in bright light

Don't buy cheap filters—they degrade image sharpness. Stick to Hoya, B+W, or Tiffen.

SD Cards, Batteries & External Mics That Work

We touched on SD cards and batteries earlier, but let's expand:

Charging Tip:

Avoid 3rd-party batteries with bad reviews—they may not show accurate charge levels.

Safe alternatives: Wasabi Power (Canon-compatible), Watson, or Canon OEM.

Microphone Upgrade (for Better Audio)

The R100 has a mic input but no headphone jack—so test audio visually or on playback.

Options That Work Well:

- Rode VideoMicro (compact, no battery needed)

- Deity V-Mic D4 Mini

- BOYA BY-MM1 (budget-friendly and solid for $30)

These improve sound dramatically over built-in mics, especially outdoors.

What's Overkill or Just Marketing Gimmickry?

Let's be honest—some accessories are more about looking "pro" than actually improving your photography.

- **Lens hoods for the kit lens** – Not needed unless shooting in super bright outdoor conditions

- **Camera cage rigs** – Unnecessary unless doing serious filmmaking

- **Cleaning pens with mystery fluid** – Stick with microfiber cloth and a blower

- **Overstuffed "Starter Bundles" on Amazon** – Often filled with low-quality items you'll never use

- **"Zoom" filters or macro lens adapters** – Typically poor quality; better to save for a real lens

Remember: You don't need to "look pro" to take beautiful, meaningful photos.

Budget-Friendly Bundles vs. Premium Picks

You may see tempting bundles that include "50-in-1 accessories" for a fraction of the cost of name-brand gear.

What to know:

- **Many bundle items are low-quality.** The tripod might wobble. The SD card might be slow.

- **Buy only what you truly need**—and get it right the first time.

Best Approach:

- Start with your core needs: SD card, spare battery, tripod, mic

- Upgrade your lens and strap once you know your style

- When in doubt: Buy once, cry never (invest in gear that lasts)

Final Thoughts: Build Your Kit with Intention

Photography is deeply personal. So your accessory kit should reflect *your* lifestyle—not someone else's gear list.

If you shoot travel and family? Go lightweight and portable.

If you're exploring portraits? Invest in great lenses and a solid tripod.

If you're just starting out? Keep it simple. Use what you have. Upgrade with purpose.

The Canon EOS R100 is powerful right out of the box. The right accessories just make it easier to express yourself, stay prepared, and create confidently in any situation.

Choose gear that solves real problems—not ones that create more clutter.

You don't need *everything*. You just need *enough to get going—and growing*.

MUST-HAVE GEAR FOR BEGINNERS

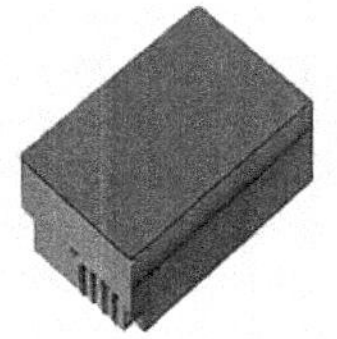 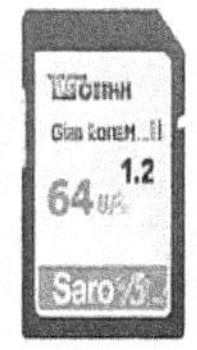 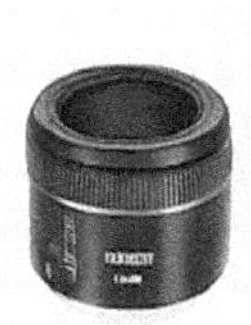

✓ **Spare battery**
At least 1 extra

✓ **UHS-1 SDC1CAR**
(at least 64 GB

✓ **Lightweight tripod**
✓ Comfortable
camera strap

TRIPODS, LENSES, AND FILTERS THAT MAKE A DIFFERENCE

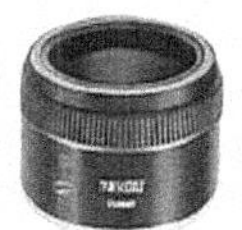 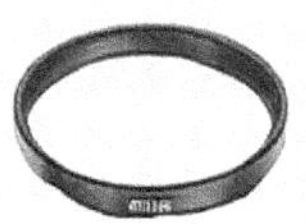 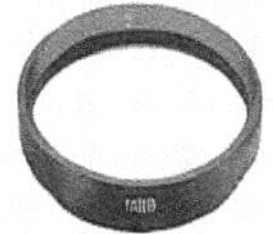

✓ **Prime lens**
Canon 50mn/f 1.8
For portraits

✓ **UV filter**
Basic lens
protection

✓ **SD cards, batteries**
Compact mics
(Rode, Deity v others)

SD CARDS, BATTERIES & EXTERNAL MICS THAT WORK

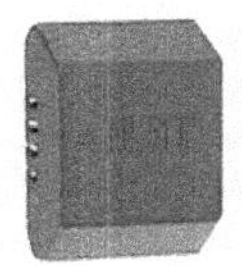 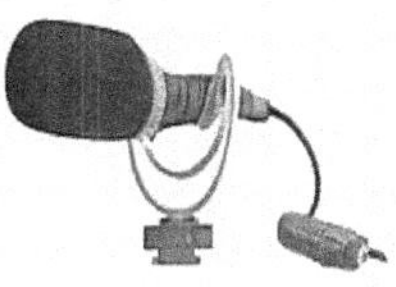 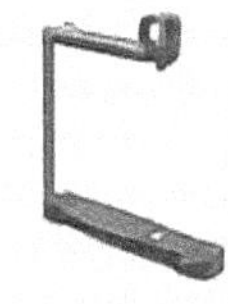 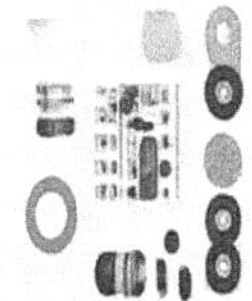

✓ **Extra LP-E17**
Battery

✓ **Compact shotgun**
Microphones
(Rode, Deity, & more)

✕ **Stick**

✕ **Gimmicky**
add-ons

APPENDIX

Your Quick-Access Canon R100 Companion

For when you need answers fast, clarity without tech jargon, and the kind of cheat sheets that make everything finally click.

Quick Setup Cheat Sheet

Just got your Canon EOS R100? Here's a no-fluff checklist to get you from box to beautiful shots:

1. **Charge the Battery** (LP-E17)

   o   Use the official charger

   o   Full charge = ~2 hours

2. **Insert SD Card (UHS-I, Class 10 or higher)**

   o   Gold contacts face the lens side

   o   64GB is a safe starting point

3. **Attach Lens**

   o   Line up the white square (lens) with white dot (body)

   o   Twist clockwise until it clicks

4. **Power On & Set:**

   o   Date/Time/Time Zone

   o   Language (English or your preference)

5. Turn Mode Dial to [A+] (Scene Intelligent Auto)

6. Point, Frame, and Press the Shutter

You're ready to shoot!

Recommended Default Settings for Beginners

Skip the guessing. These settings give you solid results across most everyday scenarios:

General Photography:

- **Mode:** [A+] (Auto) or [CA] (Creative Assist)

- **Image Quality:** JPEG Fine (Large)

- **Autofocus:** Face+Tracking

- **Drive Mode:** One-Shot AF

- **Metering:** Evaluative

- **White Balance:** Auto

- **Picture Style:** Standard

Video:

- **Mode:** Movie Auto Exposure

- **Recording Size:** FHD 30p or 60p

- **Sound Recording:** Auto (or External Mic)

- **Autofocus Method:** Movie Servo AF with Face Tracking

Canon R100 Menu Map (Plain English Visual Overview)

The Canon EOS R100 menu isn't endless—but it can feel that way if you don't know where to look. Here's a breakdown of the tabs and what they do (simplified):

Shooting Menu (Red Tabs):

- Image Quality

- ISO Speed Settings

- White Balance

- AF Operation

- Drive Mode

- Movie Recording Size

Setup Menu (Yellow Tabs):

- Date/Time

- Wi-Fi/Bluetooth

- Auto Power Off

- File Numbering

- Sensor Cleaning

My Menu (Green Tab):

- Your custom menu for favorite settings (add Image Quality, Format Card, etc.)

Tip: Spend 5 minutes creating a My Menu tab—it'll save you hours later.

FAQs from R100 Forums and User Feedback

Why are my photos blurry?

- Check autofocus is set to Face+Tracking or One-Shot

- Use faster shutter speed for moving subjects

- Hold camera steady or use a tripod

My SD card shows an error. What do I do?

- Reformat in-camera (Menu > Tools > Format Card)

- Use a fast, branded card (Class 10 or UHS-I)

- Avoid removing card while camera is still on

How long can I shoot video?

- Up to 29 minutes 59 seconds per clip

- Beware of overheating on long recordings

- Use FHD 1080p for best balance of quality and performance

Can I shoot RAW and JPEG together?

- Yes. Set image quality to RAW + JPEG in the Shooting Menu

Does the Canon R100 have image stabilization?

- Not in the body. Rely on IS-enabled lenses (like the kit 18–45mm)

Canon EOS R100 Specs (Explained in Plain English)

No jargon—just what you actually need to know.

Feature	What It Means
Sensor	24.1MP APS-C (great detail, DSLR-level quality)

Image Processor	DIGIC 8 (fast, clean images, good in low light)
ISO Range	100–12800 (expandable to 25600 for low light)
Video	Full HD 1080p at 60fps (no 4K)
Autofocus	Dual Pixel CMOS AF with Eye Tracking
Screen	Fixed 3.0" LCD (not flip-out)
Viewfinder	0.39" OLED EVF (bright and clear)
Burst Mode	6.5fps (great for action shots)
Connectivity	Wi-Fi and Bluetooth built-in
Battery	LP-E17 (up to ~400 shots per charge)
Lens Mount	RF Mount (also supports EF lenses with adapter)

Translation: You've got a compact, easy-to-use powerhouse that punches far above its weight for stills and video.

Glossary of Photography Terms (Non-Techie Version)

This isn't dictionary stuff. This is the "explain-it-like-I'm-five" version:

- **Aperture (f/stop)** – Controls how much light enters the lens. Lower number (like f/1.8) = more light + blurry background.

- **Shutter Speed** – How fast your photo is taken. Fast = freeze motion. Slow = motion blur.

- **ISO** – Camera's sensitivity to light. Higher ISO = brighter image in low light—but also more grain.

- **Exposure** – The overall brightness of your image, based on aperture + shutter + ISO.

- **Autofocus (AF)** – The camera automatically finding sharp focus.

- o   One-Shot = for still subjects

  - o   Servo AF = for moving subjects

- **White Balance** – Tells the camera what "white" looks like. Fixes weird color casts (like yellowish indoor photos).

- **RAW vs. JPEG** – RAW = full quality, big files, great for editing. JPEG = smaller, ready to share.

- **Bokeh** – That dreamy blurred background in portraits. You get it with wide apertures (like f/2.8 or lower).

- **Depth of Field** – How much of your photo is in focus. Shallow = blurred background. Deep = all sharp.

- **EVF (Electronic Viewfinder)** – What you look through on mirrorless cameras to compose your shot. Shows you a preview of exposure, color, etc.

Final Word: Keep This Appendix Close

Whether you're on your second shoot or your hundredth, this Appendix is your lifeline when questions pop up or settings get confusing.

Photography is a journey of seeing, adjusting, learning—and often, Googling. But now you've got something better: a trustworthy cheat sheet built for you, the real-life user, who wants to understand just enough to feel in control without needing a tech degree.

Use this section like a map, a compass, and a friend who's just a few steps ahead. The Canon EOS R100 is a brilliant tool. But *you* are the storyteller. And this guide? It's here to help you tell it beautifully, confidently, and clearly.

Acknowledgments

Creating this guide has been a journey made possible by more than just technical know-how—it's been powered by community, curiosity, and countless moments behind the lens.

First, to the everyday photographers—beginners, seniors, travelers, vloggers, and creators—who inspired this book: thank you. Your questions, frustrations, and breakthroughs shaped every chapter and reminded me why clarity matters.

To the online communities, forum contributors, and real-world Canon EOS R100 users who openly shared their challenges and insights: your stories breathed realism into this work.

A special thanks to my editorial team, design collaborators, and research assistants for helping bring structure, precision, and visual support to every page.

Finally, to the readers picking up this book—whether you're just unboxing your Canon R100 or finally ready to leave auto mode behind—thank you for trusting this guide as part of your journey. May it help you create images that not only look beautiful, but feel meaningful.

Keep shooting. Keep learning. The world is waiting through your lens.

About The Author

Randy Osborn is a trusted name in the world of camera education, known for transforming complex gear manuals into simple, step-by-step guides that anyone can understand. With over a decade of experience working hands-on with leading camera systems—from Sony and Canon to Nikon, Leica, and more—Randy has helped thousands of photographers, content creators, and everyday users get the most out of their cameras without the overwhelm.

Driven by a passion for accessible learning, Randy creates user-friendly books that strip away the jargon and focus on real-world usage. Whether you're shooting your first vlog, learning manual mode for the first time, or simply trying to take better family photos, Randy's guides are designed to make every setting click.

Each book combines clear instruction, practical tips, and

relatable language, making it easy for beginners and seasoned hobbyists alike to master their gear and capture life with confidence.

When he's not writing, Randy enjoys field testing new camera releases, hosting beginner-friendly workshops, and exploring hidden photography gems across the globe.

Join the journey to sharper skills and smarter shooting— one page at a time.